ARCHIBALD WAVELL

LEADERSHIP ▪ STRATEGY ▪ CONFLICT

JON DIAMOND ▪ ILLUSTRATED BY PETER DENNIS

First published in Great Britain in 2012 by Osprey Publishing,
Midland House, West Way, Botley, Oxford OX2 0PH, UK
44-02 23rd St, Suite 219, Long Island City, NY 11101, USA

E-mail: info@ospreypublishing.com

OSPREY PUBLISHING IS PART OF THE OSPREY GROUP

A CIP catalogue record for this book is available from the British Library.

ISBN: 978 1 84908 737 7
PDF E-book ISBN: 978 1 84908 738 4
E-Pub ISBN: 978 1 78096 870 4

Editorial by Ilios Publishing Ltd, Oxford, UK (www.iliospublishing.com)
Page layout by The Black Spot
Index by Mike Parkin
Typeset in Stone Serif and Officina Sans
Maps by Mapping Specialists Ltd
Originated by PDQ Digital Media Solutions Ltd, Suffolk
Printed in China through Worldprint Ltd.

12 13 14 15 16 10 9 8 7 6 5 4 3 2 1

Imperial War Museum Collections

The photographs in this book come from the Imperial War Museum's
huge collections, which cover all aspects of conflict involving Britain
and the Commonwealth since the start of the 20th century. These
rich resources are available online to search, browse and buy at
www.iwmcollections.org.uk. In addition to collections online, you
can visit the visitor rooms where you can explore over 8 million
photographs, thousands of hours of moving images, the largest sound
archive of its kind in the world, thousands of diaries and letters written
by people in wartime and a huge reference library. To make an
appointment, call (020) 7416 5320, or e-mail mail@iwm.org.uk.

www.iwm.org.uk

Artist's note

Readers may care to note that the original paintings from which the
colour plates in this book were prepared are available for private sale.
The Publishers retain all reproduction copyright whatsoever. All
enquiries should be addressed to:

Peter Dennis, Fieldhead, the Park, Mansfield, NOTTS, NG18 2AT, UK

The Publishers regret that they can enter into no correspondence upon
this matter.

Front cover image

© Getty images

The Woodland Trust

Osprey Publishing are supporting the Woodland Trust, the UK's leading
woodland conservation charity, by funding the dedication of trees.

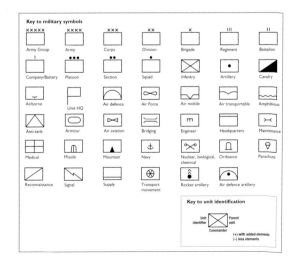

CONTENTS

INTRODUCTION

Archibald Wavell (1883–1950) is one of the few great commanders throughout history to have combined the keen intellect of the scholar, the artistic passion of a poet, having compiled *Other Men's Flowers*, and a historian's understanding of the level of military science of his time. In addition, Wavell also possessed a cunning innovativeness with regard to applying new technologies to the continually developing art of warfare, along with the insight and character judgement to identify many protégés. These junior officers would refine Wavell's ideas and then implement their upgraded methods, such as 'all-arms' warfare, guerrilla tactics and strategic deception under his patient tutelage. Wavell was an ardent believer in the unorthodox methods of making war, with his experiences on General Sir Edmund Allenby's staff in Palestine during World War I providing the source of much of his inspiration.

Wavell, as C-in-C, India, planning the Arakan Offensive with staff officers on the Assam/Burma border in December 1942. (IWM, IND 1525)

Despite Wavell's conceptual and battlefield breakthroughs, he never forgot his regimental roots in the Black Watch and the vital role of the infantryman. Nor did he overlook his experiences during World War I, which reinforced his respect for the ordinary infantryman. As he stated, 'Let us be clear about three facts: first, all battles and all wars are won in the end by the infantryman. Secondly, the infantryman always bears the brunt. His casualties are heavier, he suffers greater extremes of discomfort and fatigue than the other arms. Thirdly, the art of the infantryman is less stereotyped and far harder to acquire in modern war than that of any other arm.' Wavell's passion for

Field Marshal Wavell working at his desk in Delhi as Viceroy of India. (IWM, IB2)

military deception and secrecy, as well as his introduction of state-of-the-art weaponry and tactics, were all designed to ensure the greatest success with the fewest casualties for his beloved infantry. Not only was Wavell an excellent trainer of troops, both during peacetime and on the battlefield, but, according to his biographer John Connell he possessed a special insight into the 'ideas and feelings of the private soldiers and subaltern officers' who fought under his leadership and direction.

In July 1939, Wavell was named General Officer Commanding-in-Chief (GOC-in-C) of Middle East Command, with the rank of full general. Few great commanders have been given the task of campaigning across such a vast stretch of territory with a military apparatus that was both antiquated and underdeveloped, owing to neglect and under-funding, along with understrength troop numbers. These were the daunting tasks facing Wavell, who between June 1940 and June 1941 was the only British theatre commander actively engaging the Axis enemy forces. His Middle East arena comprised the Western Desert (Egypt and Cyrenaica), East Africa, Greece, Crete, Syria and Iraq. No other Allied commander during World War II would have such a list of often-simultaneous operations. All of his campaigns were of unqualified difficulty owing to logistical deficiencies in the British Army, as well as the other arms, at this time of the war. Wavell, the eternal pragmatic and modest analyst, commented on this arduous campaign record 'some have been successful, others have failed'.

The 12 months from June 1940 to June 1941 witnessed the British Expeditionary Force (BEF) being expelled from the Continent via a series of evacuations, most notably at Dunkirk. The British Isles themselves were preparing hastily for the threat of a Nazi invasion, Operation *Seelöwe*. The sky over south-eastern England was the scene of a vicious air-battle between the Royal Air Force (RAF) and the vaunted Luftwaffe. Cities within the United Kingdom were mercilessly bombed, with London subjected to the several-month-long Blitz. The oceans and seas surrounding the British Isles were subjected to the U-boat terror. If ever there was a time for a commander to strike a blow for his country, to gain a convincing victory to uplift public morale and governmental confidence, it was now and Wavell was the only commander able to fulfil that need. It is fair to state that Wavell's victories were against the Italians, Vichy French and pro-German Arab revolutionaries, and that when combatting the German Wehrmacht his campaigns often ended with disastrous consequences. However, one needs to remember that from June 1940 up to June 1941, Britain had no ally and the telling effect of the appeasement years on the British Army's lack of preparation cannot be overemphasized.

Unlike some other British generals, who rapidly advanced to major commands from relative or virtual obscurity through a combination of well-positioned mentors and serendipity, Wavell's pre-war career was noteworthy for a varied number of command positions. In fact, if it were not for a matter of circumstance he might have achieved the premier rank within the British Army, Chief of the Imperial General Staff (CIGS), in 1937. Again, in contrast to other British generals during World War II, Wavell possessed a strong streak of humility, which some claim may have led him to rate some of his own best qualities lower than others did. Perhaps this facet of his personality may have contributed to his 'famous and formidable silences'. He clearly did not suffer fools or bombastic contemporaries gladly, but rather than argue he often remained quiet. At times, this reticent stance incurred the wrath of his 'imperious political master', Prime Minister Winston Churchill. Wavell's unspoken style when confronted by the Prime Minister's challenges or reprimands ultimately caused Churchill, perhaps without merit, to lose confidence in him. Whereas other British generals, such as Montgomery and Slim, clearly won over their subordinate officers with their glib or constructive style, Wavell has been accused of being aloof. However, these same officers remembered Wavell's stalwart presence, albeit unstated, so that they affectionately referred to him as 'The Chief'.

THE EARLY YEARS

Archibald Wavell was born on 5 May 1883 at Colchester, the only son of Major Archibald Graham Wavell, an officer in the Norfolk Regiment in the British Army. His grandfather served in the East India Company's Bengal Army and the family origins trace back to Norman stock that lived near the bay of Vauville on the Cherbourg peninsula. Upon migrating to England, Wavell's ancestors resided in Hampshire for centuries, with a progressive Anglicization of the family name Vauville to Wavell.

Wavell's father served for 28 years in the Norfolk Regiment, which after 1888 was stationed in Gibraltar and India. Young Archibald Wavell thus spent the early years of his life at an army barracks in India, which left an everlasting impression on him with regard to the British Army in India and the Raj. Not many youths spend their childhood years in situations where, in the future, they would ultimately be called upon to be leaders. But so it was for Wavell, who was to become C-in-C, India, and later Governor-General and Viceroy of India. In 1891 his father took an exchange commission in the Black Watch, which, too, was going to have ramifications for young Archibald's future in the British Army. Wavell grew up within the close-knit circle of the Black Watch or as some would refer to it, as 'a son of the regiment'. In 1894, Colonel Wavell left the command of his battalion in the Black Watch and from there went to a staff appointment and then for three-and-a-half years command of the 42nd Regimental District, a recruiting centre at Perth. In July 1898, Colonel Wavell took a staff appointment at the War Office.

Wavell aged 15 as a student at Winchester. (Wavell Estate)

At the age of 10, Wavell entered Summer Fields, a preparatory school at Oxford. He was described as 'sturdily built, a little under height for his age, a quiet, composed and resolute boy'. Even at that young age he was known for 'keeping his own counsel', which would also impact upon his command years during World War II. In 1896, Wavell was one of the Summer Fields students who won scholarships to public schools; he got into Winchester College. His ancestors had a long tradition at the college; there had been 11 Wavells in attendance as students between 1478 and 1930. During the 17th and 18th centuries, some of the Wavell clan served as mayors of Winchester. He made friends at Winchester, although some died in France during World War I, Wavell was to lament later on in life, 'No wonder we lacked leadership in the postwar years'.

At Winchester, Wavell studied hard and was particularly keen on memorizing verses of poetry. His teachers awarded him good grades; however, a Second Master wrote that, 'he must be a little more communicative as he grows older'. Although he had excelled in the humanities and classics, Wavell made the decision to join the Army Class at Winchester, despite another of his teachers stating that 'he would probably have a brilliant career before him at the University'. However, Wavell was quite analytical about his choice of the Army Class: 'I never felt any special inclination to a military career, but it would have taken more independence of character than I possessed at the time to avoid it. Nearly all my relations were in the Army. I had been brought up amongst soldiers; and my father, while professing to give me complete liberty of choice, was determined that I should be a soldier. I had no particular bent towards any other profession, and I took the line of least resistance.'

The Boer War began in October 1899 when Wavell, a 16 year-old, was still at Winchester. In December 1899, Wavell received the bad news of the defeat of the Highland Brigade at the battle of Magersfontein, with many officers and other ranks of the Black Watch killed in action. Wavell knew and admired them as only a son of the regiment milling around the barracks could. In January 1900, Wavell's father, aged 57 and now a major-general, was dispatched to South Africa to command the 15th Brigade. He performed well at Bloemfontein but contracted enteric fever and eventually returned to England in October 1900 just as his 17-year-old son passed examinations for the Royal Military Academy, Sandhurst.

Although there appears to be no family or childhood trauma affecting young Archibald Wavell, of the sort some of his contemporaries suffered from, a lingering concern about his lack of communication seems to have followed him. Perhaps the spartan life and scholarly ambience of Winchester College pushed Wavell to favour his natural tendency towards introspection. As many stressed, although young Archibald was quiet, no one doubted his intellectual capacity. The Second Master, Mr M. J. Rendall, 'a brilliant and gregarious extrovert' at Winchester, wrote to Mrs Wavell upon her son's departure from the College: 'I congratulate him on his very good place in the Sandhurst list; he has undoubted ability and has worked well. I hope in the future he will come out of his shell; he was too retiring here; probably the Army will do this for him. I saw less of him than I should have liked, but his work lay on other lines. Of his character I think very well; it was nothing that was not honourable and gentlemanly.'

Wavell's father, now home from South Africa, became a staff officer to the Commander-in-Chief in Ireland, HRH the Duke of Connaught. Clearly the elder Wavell had a successful and rich military career with battalion command in the Black Watch, many promotions and distinguished service during wartime. The younger Wavell, now embarking for Sandhurst, was clearly going to have 'big shoes to fill' as he followed in his father's (and grandfather's) professional paths as a soldier.

THE MILITARY LIFE, 1900–40

Wavell spent only one year at Sandhurst since, in order to generate more junior officers owing to casualties suffered in the Boer Wars, the curriculum had to be cut short. Although his grades at Sandhurst were considered average, his conduct report was exemplary with Gentleman Cadet Wavell ranked first on the merit order for his two terms at Sandhurst. Wavell evaluated his own performance at Sandhurst with humility: 'The book work gave me no trouble, but I was not good at the drill nor at field sketching, which was at that time considered a necessary qualification for an officer.... As I had no talent for either map-making or drill, I was never promoted.' He was commissioned on 8 May 1901, only three days after his 18th birthday.

Since both regular battalions of the Black Watch were deployed overseas, Wavell spent two months with several other subalterns with the Details of the Black Watch, a recruits' drill course at Edinburgh Castle. The stocky, sturdy Wavell earned the sobriquet 'Podgy', which stayed with him until he returned to the regiment after World War I. A biographer noted that although 'his own service in and deep and abiding connections with the Black Watch were to mould his outlook and his character,... there was hardly a drop of Scots blood in his veins'. After acquiring rifle-shooting skills in England, followed by a month's leave, the Black Watch's new recruits and officers were sent to South Africa for active service on 29 September 1901. Wavell was one of three subalterns with the group. After being shipped to Durban, this group was sent by rail to the Transvaal, where its active service battalions were fighting mounted Boer commandos. As Wavell remembered, 'Not very exciting work, but it taught a young officer his job on active service, how to handle and look after his men, and himself'. His battalion's column was tasked with the capture of the remaining Boers in his area. His diary entry for 28 February was, 'End of drive, 1,100 Boers snaffled'. Wavell stayed in South Africa for almost exactly a year before being given leave to return to England.

Wavell at the age of 27 as a subaltern in the Black Watch. He spent his childhood years growing up in his father's regiment, and never forgot his regimental roots. (Wavell Estate)

At the end of February 1903, Wavell sailed for India to rejoin his battalion stationed at Ambala. Subsequently, the 2nd Battalion of the Black Watch was transferred to the North-West Frontier. His five years' service on the subcontinent left a permanent impression on how he viewed the Army and the Empire. In a moment of introspection, Wavell noted, 'I was quite a good subaltern, and probably did more work than most.... I found my feet with my brother officers, and I think learned to handle men quite reasonably well. But I was never really a leader and was quite content to go with the common opinion and practice.' In February 1904, while in India, he was promoted to the temporary rank of lieutenant.

While serving in a staff capacity away from his regiment at Divisional Headquarters in Rawalpindi in February 1908, he came across a telegram requesting a British subaltern officer to command the ammunition column of the Bazar Valley expedition, which was about to set out to confront the Pathans during a recent outbreak of hostilities along the frontier. A requirement for this posting was to have passed Higher Standard Urdu, a language in which Wavell, unlike many of his fellow officers, had achieved proficiency.

In 1908, after coming first in entrance examinations following an intensive two-month period of study, Wavell entered the Staff College, Camberley, upon the advice of his father rather than applying for a posting with the King's African Rifles. He received one of the only two 'A' grades awarded, which was even more praiseworthy since he was the youngest student of his group during his two-year tenure. At the Staff College, Wavell made an observation that would become pertinent to his later command experience in the barren North African desert: 'The instruction... was still to my mind too academic and theoretical and aimed too high.... What seemed

Wavell's mentor from World War I, General Sir Edmund Allenby. Wavell learned the cardinal principles of deception, secrecy and surprise while serving under him in Palestine. (IWM, Q 82969)

to me weak was the administrative side, especially supply and transport. It was never rubbed into us that all operations were entirely dependent on transportation.'

Before leaving Staff College, its new commandant, Major-General Sir William Robertson, recommended that Wavell go to Russia as a language student. In 1911, he spent a year in Imperial Russia observing the Tsar's Army in its manoeuvres and also learning Russian, qualifying as a First Class Interpreter in the process. In the years that followed, Wavell worked as a General Staff Officer (GSO) III in the Russian Section in the War Office, being appointed acting captain in March 1912. He wrote a handbook on the Russian Army and made two more trips to the Russian Army's annual manoeuvres. Wavell's status as a military intellectual was becoming clear to Major-General Henry Wilson, who served as Commandant of the Staff College during Wavell's first year and would become both a field marshal and CIGS. These trips enabled Wavell to observe first-hand the deployment of a large military force in the field, an experience that most British officers could only dream of.

With the outbreak of World War I, Wavell was temporarily placed in command of Section 5 of the Directorate of Military Operations at the War Office, but yearned for a battlefield command. On 12 September 1914, within weeks of the outbreak of war, Wavell wrote in his diary: 'I think I'm complete now with everything for the field, except orders to go. I'm feeling too utterly depressed and really don't care what happens, one will never be able to make up for having missed this last month. I wish I'd never gone near the Staff College or Russia.' However, within weeks of his despondent diary entry, he was appointed brigade-major in the 9th Infantry Brigade, which was fighting on the Western Front in France. Wavell insisted on personally inspecting the battalions of his brigade in the trenches regularly in order to address his troops' requirements. He was always searching for ways to improve the lot of the infantryman, and neither sought to squander their lives nor accrue needless casualties. To this end, Wavell frequently reconnoitred the battlefield not only to improve the layout of his brigade's position but also to update map coordinates to ensure proper artillery support and assistance.

In June 1915, Captain Wavell became personally and directly involved in the carnage of the Western Front when he was wounded at the battle of Second Ypres. His brigade had led an assault on Bellewaarde Ridge and during the attack a splinter from a German shell destroyed his left eye. The 9th Infantry Brigade lost 73 officers out of 96 and 2,012 men out of 3,663 in the battle of Bellewaarde Ridge, and the experience was a formative one for Wavell, who became convinced that the British tactics of the day, involving massed frontal assaults by infantry across no man's land against strongly held defensive positions cordoned with barbed wire and manned by machine-gunners, were futile. He envisaged instead employing specially trained troops, using stealth and transport for heightened mobility, to take part in offensive operations where unorthodoxy would be the rule. This was not the universal response to the situation on the Western Front, and as late as 1933 Wavell was still in the process of convincing his tradition-bound military leaders 'to shake the last of the Flanders mud out of our minds' and embrace new forms of warfare to limit casualties and prevent a repetition of the senseless slaughter of the Western Front.

After convalescence and a staff appointment to the 64th Highland Division in Scotland, Wavell returned to France as a GSO II (Staff Duties). He was promoted to major on 8 May 1916 and subsequently posted as a liaison officer to the Russian Army of the Caucasus by the CIGS, General Sir William Robertson, one of his commandants at Camberley. With a local rank of lieutenant-colonel, Wavell reported on the Turkish Army facing the Russians in the Caucasus, and his reports proved highly influential in the development of the British war effort in Mesopotamia and Palestine. After the Bolshevik uprising in Russia, Wavell returned to London in June 1917, being given a brevet rank of lieutenant-colonel at the age of 34.

In June 1917, Robertson appointed Wavell as his personal liaison officer with General Sir Edmund Allenby, now Commander-in-Chief of the Egyptian Expeditionary Force. In this role, Wavell served in Palestine alongside both Allenby and T. E. Lawrence – an experience that further developed his thinking on warfare. Wavell entered Jerusalem in December 1917 and advanced to Damascus at the side of both of these soon-to-be military giants. Wavell regarded Allenby as his mentor and model for the rest of his life, carefully learning the twin tactics of surprise and deception which assisted in Allenby's victories over the Turks at Beersheba and Megiddo in 1918. He also learned about the art of command in a desert theatre, and the importance of sound operational planning and careful attention to logistics, in which Allenby excelled. It was his mentor's great victory in the battle of Third Gaza that conclusively demonstrated to Wavell the importance of water, transport and surprise in any desert conflict. Wavell was a devoted follower of Allenby, writing a two-volume biography of him as well as penning a historical treatise about the Palestine campaign. The campaign served only to strengthen his opinions about the important role that the infantry could play: 'A study of what well-trained troops, capable of manoeuvre, were able to accomplish may serve as a corrective to the pessimism as to the offensive power of infantry which the experience of rigid trench warfare in France engendered in the minds of some.'

Prior to the end of the conflict, Wavell held a number of positions including Assistant Adjutant and Quartermaster General of the British Delegation to the Supreme Allied War Council in Versailles and later Brigadier-General, General Staff (BGGS) of the newly formed XXII Corps. After XXII Corps was disbanded in March 1918, as a new German offensive was beginning along the Western Front, Wavell was selected as BGGS of

XX Corps. He served in this capacity from April 1918 to March 1920, following which he returned to England.

One character trait that was honed by his World War I experience was his unwillingness to engage with those who did not interest him, instead remaining silent. This, combined with a growing distaste for the interference of politicians in military dealings did not bode well for the success of his future relationship with Winston Churchill.

The inter-war period

Upon returning to England, Wavell returned to regimental duty with the 2nd Battalion the Black Watch, with the rank of brevet lieutenant-colonel. The initial half of 1921 was spent in Germany as a company commander before he was promoted to colonel. After a brief stint as Assistant Adjutant General (AAG) in the War Office, Wavell became GSO I (Chief of Staff) of Military Operations in 1923, responsible for Imperial Defence and Strategy. Sprinkled amidst these assignments were intense periods of reading military history, writing and lecturing.

Amid periods of underemployment and half pay, Wavell was appointed, in 1926, as GSO I of the 3rd Division and worked on an experimental mechanized force, which was to dominate some of his thoughts, specifically, 'the requirements of mobility, fire-power, and armour… that tanks would need dismounted infantry for protection, and that wireless communications should be further developed to support future armoured forces operating over hitherto undreamt-of distances'. Clearly, Wavell at this point, was light years ahead of his 'hide-bound' contemporaries and demonstrated a keen and intuitive conceptual understanding about armour's role in any future conflict.

Later appointments included GOC 6th Infantry Brigade in the 2nd Division from 1930 to 1934. In 1931, Wavell was given a new brigade major, Eric Dorman-Smith, who, like Wavell, had been wounded and decorated while serving with the 9th Infantry Brigade at the battle of Bellewaarde Ridge. Barrie Pitt in *Crucible of War* describes Dorman-Smith as 'concealing a fertile and original mind… with a cutting wit and an impatience with orthodox doctrine unleavened by imagination and administered by seniority, which had already earned him enemies in high places and would continue to do so.' However, Wavell and Dorman-Smith were able to 'produce new, and now legendary, training exercises designed to enhance realism and to hold the interest of the soldiers'. For these efforts, the brigade was renamed the 6th (Experimental) Infantry Brigade. Night marches followed by early dawn attacks, as well as behind-the-lines assaults on enemy headquarters were some of the new tactics explored through the planning and testing devised by Wavell and his protégé, Dorman-Smith.

Wavell was promoted to major-general in October 1933, largely due to the success of the Experimental Brigade. In March 1935, Wavell became GOC 2nd Division, and in September 1937 he was appointed GOC Palestine, succeeding his friend Liutenant-General Sir John Dill. At that time, the Arab

Revolt was under way and Wavell met an unorthodox artilleryman, Captain Orde Wingate. Wavell authorized him to raise the Jewish irregular Special Night Squads to collect intelligence and subject the Arab guerrillas to active harassment. Wavell always had a penchant for the unexpected tactic and was to make use of Wingate's unorthodox approaches both in Abyssinia in 1940 and Burma in 1943–44. Other junior officers cultivated by Wavell in Palestine included Richard O'Connor, Dudley Clarke, Ralph Bagnold and Tony Simonds.

Wavell assumed his appointment as GOC, Southern Command, in April 1938. At this time, Wavell was in the running to be selected as the next CIGS by the Secretary of State for War Leslie Hore-Belisha; however, the position went to Lord Gort instead. Nonetheless, his service at Southern Command position was highly endorsed by Captain Basil Liddell Hart, military correspondent for *The Times*, who referred to Wavell as 'one of the two soldiers in our Army who were potentially *great* commanders', the other being General Sir John Dill. Wavell's time at Southern Command was brief and he became GOC-in-C, Middle East Command, in July 1939, arriving in Cairo on 2 August 1939 just before the outbreak of World War II in Europe.

THE HOUR OF DESTINY

Commander-in-Chief, Middle East Command

In 1939, Wavell received a letter from an old friend, George Giffard, Military Secretary at the War Office, asking if he would like to be considered for the appointment of GOC-in-C of the newly formed Middle East Command. Wavell had anticipated that if war broke out, he would become Commander II Corps in the BEF. Wavell was actually inclined towards the Middle East Command for a variety of reasons. First, he wanted a theatre where a repetition of the Continental trench warfare with its ensuing slaughter was unlikely. Second, his previous active service in the Middle East in World War I and the inter-war period made him acutely aware just how important this theatre would be in a future conflict. Third, he would be walking in the footsteps of his mentor, General Sir Edmund Allenby, who won fame and glory in Palestine upon being transferred from the Western Front. Fourth, Wavell would be able to build his own ideas and tactics and add the element of true mobility in the wide-open, expansive desert.

So Wavell departed for Cairo on 27 July 1939 with glowing praise from the *Daily Telegraph*, which proclaimed that 'no better choice than that of Sir Archibald Wavell [recently knighted] could have been made'. Little did Wavell know that his 'hour of destiny' would comprise a four-year period of unending work, ceaseless travelling and simultaneous campaigns that would have provided a formidable challenge for any commander.

On 31 July 1939, Wavell wrote an appreciation for the CIGS about the role of the Middle East Command:

> The last war was won in the West.... The next war will be won or lost in the Mediterranean; and the longer it takes us to secure effective control of the Mediterranean, the harder will the winning of the war be. The task of the Staff of the Middle East Command is therefore to plan, in conjunction with the other Services, not merely the defence of Egypt and our other interests in the Middle East, but such measures of offence as will enable us and our Allies to dominate the Mediterranean at the earliest possible moment; and thereafter to take the counter-offensive against Germany in Eastern and S.E. Europe.

This assessment proved to be an accurate prediction of the actual course of events from December 1940 to July 1943.

The Western Desert and East Africa

Established in the summer of 1939, Wavell's Middle East Command encompassed nine countries and parts of two continents, an area 1,700 by 2,000 miles (2,700 by 3,200km). He commanded all British land forces in Egypt, the Sudan, Palestine, Transjordan and Cyprus, and with the outbreak of war his responsibilities increased to include Aden, Iraq, British Somaliland and the shores of the Persian Gulf. Wavell's duties were not only to prepare war plans for the entire theatre, but to reinforce critical fronts strategically and act as a 'quartermaster-in-chief', distributing troops and supplies to his many garrisons. Additionally, Wavell was to consult with his naval and air counterparts as well as meet with His Majesty's ambassadors in Egypt and Iraq, the Governor-General in the Sudan, the High Commissioner for Palestine and Transjordan, as well as the Governors of Cyprus, Aden and British Somaliland. The diplomatic and political aspects of Wavell's

LRDG 30-cwt Chevrolet trucks during a break in the desert.
(IWM, E 012385)

appointment were significant and added considerably to his command problems. For this wide range of tasks and responsibilities, Wavell was initially given a headquarters staff of only five officers.

During the 12 months between June 1940 and June 1941, Wavell planned and directly oversaw a multitude of campaigns. No single Allied commander in World War II ever undertook such a wide range of operations in terms of their military and political scope, not to mention their tactical complexity.

Leaving Siwa Oasis in May 1942, an LRDG patrol begins an operation. (IWM, E 012375)

To Wavell's west, Italy had nine divisions in Tripoli and five in Cyrenaica, comprising some 215,000 men. Against this Wavell had the 7th Armoured Division, still not up to strength in either men or vehicles and not fully trained; 21 battalions of infantry in Egypt and Palestine; two regiments of cavalry (still with their horses) and four regiments of artillery. The Duke of Aosta had another 250,000 troops under his command in Italian East Africa (Eritrea, Italian Somaliland and the recently conquered areas of Ethiopia). To confront this force, Wavell had three British infantry battalions in the Sudan, along with 20 companies of the Sudan Defence Force. In British Somaliland, there was the small force of the Sudan Camel Corps. In Kenya, there were two brigades of the King's African Rifles, while in Aden there were two Indian battalions.

Brigadier Eric-Dorman Smith, a Wavell protégé, conferring with General Sir Alan Brooke in Egypt, August 1942. (IWM, E 15298)

In order to fight the Italians after their declaration of war on Britain in June 1940, Wavell had to improvise and devise new tactics. In Egypt, he needed to keep the Italians invading from Libya off guard, while he developed an offensive to destroy them. To accomplish these tasks, he relied on some intriguing military protégés. Ralph Bagnold, creator of the Long Range Desert Group (LRDG), was a major in the Royal Corps of Signals as well as a gentleman adventurer who had pioneered desert exploration in the 1930s and made the first east–west crossing of the Libyan Desert in 1932. Bagnold was also an author of what was to become the standard

Lieutenant-Colonel Dudley Clarke, who organized deception operations in North Africa for Wavell as the head of A Force. Here, he is photographed in his female (left) and male (right) attire after having been captured by the police on an ill-fated trip to Madrid.

textbook on sand dunes, *The Physics of Blown Sand*. A World War I veteran, Bagnold was called out of retirement in August 1939 and his meeting with Wavell in the Middle East was pure serendipity. In September 1939, Bagnold was Kenya-bound for a routine posting on a troop-ship in the Mediterranean when his vessel was damaged and put into Port Said for repairs. Having served in Egypt in the 1920s and 1930s, Bagnold went to Cairo to meet friends. Wavell learned of his presence in Cairo and summoned him immediately, cancelling his posting to Kenya to keep him near by in the event of war with the Italians. This episode again demonstrates Wavell's far-sightedness. Wavell knew that if Italy declared war, he would have to fight in Libya and a man like Bagnold, who had unmatched experience in the inhospitable and often uncharted deserts of North Africa, would be a mine of information. In June 1940, following the outbreak of war, Bagnold met again with Wavell and urged him to authorize small mobile scouting forces to reconnoitre the Italians crossing from Libya into Egypt . Wavell dictated an order to heads of departments and branches that any request Bagnold might make for personnel and equipment 'should be met instantly and without question'. Bagnold's reaction to Wavell was 'What a man'!

Bagnold had developed an accurate sun compass and was able to modify Model–T Fords so that they could conserve water and traverse the dunes of the Libyan Sand Sea. Given six weeks by Wavell to recruit a desert raiding force, Bagnold sent for two of his pre-war desert-exploring companions, Bill Shaw and Pat Clayton. Bagnold also acquired 150 volunteers from the newly arrived New Zealand Division, who seemed to be more mechanically inclined than their British counterparts. This force, transported in 30-cwt Chevrolet trucks and 15-cwt command cars, carried a variety of armament to commit acts of 'desert piracy' against the Italians. Under Bagnold, the LRDG harassed the enemy throughout the North African campaign. Their hit-and-run tactics also made the British forces appear more numerous to the invading Italian Tenth Army. Finally, the LRDG would ferry and guide Lieutenant-Colonel David Stirling's Special Air Service (SAS) through the desert in their raids deep behind enemy lines against both Italian and German foes.

Again resorting to his experiences from his days on Allenby's staff in Palestine, Wavell integrated deception into his tactical repertoire and sought the expertise in this mode of warfare from another of his protégés, Dudley Clarke. Wavell, early in 1940, knew that he would require a centrally controlled and well-orchestrated system of deception, much akin to the stratagems constructed by Allenby during his conquest of the Turks. On 13 November 1940, Wavell informed London of his intent to form 'a special section of Intelligence for Deception of the enemy' and requested an officer who had served under him in Palestine in the 1930s and in whom he had 'recognized an original, unorthodox outlook on soldiering', coupled with 'originality, ingenuity, and [a] somewhat impish

British tankers disguising an M3 US tank as a truck with a 'Sunshield' decoy device devised by Clarke's A Force. (IWM, MH 20767)

sense of humour'. At this time, Wavell had already concluded that tactical deceit would need to be used to keep the Italians ignorant of the weakness of his forces until adequate numbers of troops could be assembled. Dudley Clarke was Wavell's man for this task.

On 19 December 1940, Clarke reported for duty as 'Personal Intelligence Officer (Special Duties) to the C-in-C Middle East'. Clarke's position entailed not only the planning and conduct of deception activities, but the organization and operation of a Middle Eastern equivalent of M19, the element of Military Intelligence at the War Office responsible for assisting British soldiers in evading capture, securing information from prisoners of war in enemy hands and assisting them to escape. Being less secret than deception, it served throughout the war as a cover for Clarke's primary task. His fundamental belief was that a clandestine campaign's aim was to conserve lives rather than simply inflict a maximum of enemy casualties. Clarke learned through his deception of the Duke of Aosta in British Somaliland that one must focus not on what you want the enemy to *think* but what you want him to *do*. Simply misinforming the enemy does no

To simulate tank tracks in the desert as part of a deception operation, Clarke utilized the 'Trackmaker' device. (IWM, MH 20772)

good for the deception team if, as a result of the ruse, the opposing force takes an undesirable action.

On 28 March 1941, Clarke's pioneering deception organization was officially designated A Force. On 8 April 1941, A Force moved into 6 Kasr-el-Nil, a building that also housed a brothel, where it remained until the end of the war in Europe. In a little more than a year since being given his new assignment by Wavell, he had devised the principles of operational deception – often by trial and error.

With these elements in place, Wavell was in position to oversee the winter campaigns in the Western Desert in 1940–41 (Operation *Compass*) and the campaign in East Africa over the winter and spring of 1941. These campaigns were, according to Robert Woolcombe, 'two of the most resounding military victories in history', with numerically inferior British forces annihilating their Italian adversaries.

A 1924-pattern Rolls-Royce armoured car, equipped with a Boys anti-tank rifle and a Bren gun, patrols the Egyptian frontier and harries the Italians soon after the declaration of war. (IWM, E 178)

The campaign in the Western Desert was a particularly bold step as Wavell committed two divisions that were the only force available for the defence of Egypt. The victories 'cheered and inspired the British Empire and the neutral world at a time when Axis power seemed invincible'. England needed to demonstrate that along with her Empire and the Dominions, she was not only actively engaged with the Axis forces but capable of beating them. This would help to ensure a wary United States to continue the Lend-Lease policy and justify Roosevelt's gradual, yet secret, incremental plan to ramp up its combatant status.

Wavell's decision to launch a counterattack was made after Graziani's Tenth Army halted its laborious advance into Egypt on 13 September 1940. On 21 September, Wavell issued the orders to begin the preparation for Operation *Compass*. Wavell's original intention was a 'spoiling attack' since he had multiple pressures to which his meagre forces were subjected to. Wavell issued instructions to Lieutenant-General Sir Henry Maitland Wilson, GOC, British Troops Egypt (BTE), to make an attack on the stationary positions, which Graziani was content to sit behind, in the Sofafi–Sidi Barrani–Buqbuq area. In Wavell's words, it was to be 'a short and swift operation, lasting from four to five days at the most, and taking every advantage of the element of surprise'. To maintain secrecy, Wavell added,

Wavell (left), Air Chief Marshal Sir Arthur Longmore (AOC-in-C) (centre), and Foreign Secretary Sir Anthony Eden in the Middle East in October 1940, just prior to planning Operation *Compass*. (IWM, E 802)

'I do not wish the contents of this note disclosed or the plans discussed with anyone except your Brigadier General Staff, General O'Connor, and General Creagh'. Wavell was simultaneously planning a campaign to conquer Italy's East African empire. If successful, it would eliminate the Italian presence on the Red Sea and strengthen the securing of both Kenya and the Sudan.

Richard O'Connor was Wavell's assault leader for Operation *Compass*. O'Connor was born in 1889 and educated at Sandhurst. He won several medals during World War I and commanded a brigade in Peshawar on the North-West Frontier in 1936. Two years later, he was promoted to major-general and commanded the 7th Division in southern Palestine, while also serving as Military Governor of Jerusalem during the Arab Revolt. Wavell chose O'Connor to command the Western Desert Force because he had a reputation for boldness and unorthodoxy. Certainly, mobility was paramount to O'Connor from his previous experience. The date for the start of Operation *Compass* was 9 December 1940. On 28 November, Wavell anticipating a conquest wrote, 'the difficulties, administrative and tactical, of a deep advance are fully realized. It is, however, possible that an opportunity may offer for converting the enemy's defeat into an outstanding victory.… I do wish to make certain that if a big opportunity occurs we are prepared morally, mentally and administratively to use it to the fullest.'

OPERATION *COMPASS*

For the final planning for Operation *Compass,* Wavell organized a meeting in his rather spartan office in Cairo with O'Connor and Wilson on 4 December. Maps, plans and aerial reconnaissance photographs of the terrain, as well as the Italian positions in the fortified camps of Nibeiwa and the Tummars (East and West), were reviewed in order to formulate the final operation orders to O'Connor's troops for the 'limited raid' against the now static elements of the Italian Tenth Army.

Lieutenant-General Richard O'Connor, who commanded the Western Desert Force during Operation *Compass*. At Beda Fomm, he destroyed the entire Italian Tenth Army in Cyrenaica, but ironically became a POW a short time afterwards. (IWM, E 1899)

On 26 November, under conditions of intense secrecy, a rehearsal for Operation *Compass* was conducted in the desert on a plateau south of Mersa Matruh using replicas of the Italians' camps at Nibeiwa and the Tummars. This 'dry-run' utilized a plan of attack based on orthodox lines as laid down in the official Army pamphlet, *The Division in Attack.* The evaluators of the exercise were O'Connor, Wilson, associated staff officers and Brigadier Eric Dorman-Smith, who was now the commandant of the Middle East Staff College in Haifa. Dorman-Smith had been sent up to O'Connor's forward headquarters on 25 November on the secret and personal instructions of Wavell himself. This assembly was highly critical of the training exercise, and Dorman-Smith wrote an appreciation that modified the attack plans. It was aptly entitled *A Method of Attack on an Entrenched Camp in the Desert*, and was given an extremely limited circulation in

The British XIII Corps attack, 4–7 February 1940

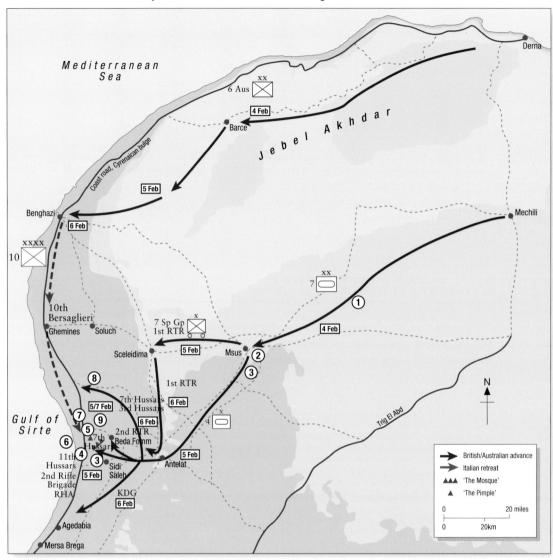

light of Wavell's requirement for secrecy about Operation *Compass*. The basis for the meeting on 4 December was to decide how best to implement the drastic modifications devised by Dorman-Smith and O'Connor.

O'Connor possessed an instinctive knowledge of mobile, light mechanized warfare, but for this attack he would use heavy infantry tanks (Matildas) of the 7th Royal Tank Regiment (RTR). Instead of the conventional method of using an artillery bombardment followed by a combined infantry and armoured advance, it was decided to use the Matilda tanks in an attack on the fortified camps first, with the infantry of the 4th Indian Division following up the armoured assault. At Nibeiwa the assault would therefore be a surprise move, unsupported by artillery, down an unmined track into the north-west (rear) corner of the camp. At the same time, other infantry were to draw the

1. On 4 February, the 4th Armoured Brigade (with A and C Sqns, 11th Hussars, in front) strikes out across the desert, along with a squadron from the King's Dragoon Guards. Behind them are tanks from three tank regiments (3rd and 7th Hussars and 2nd RTR), followed by 2nd Bn Rifle Brigade, 4th RHA, and elements of 106th RHA.
2. By 1530hrs on 4 February, the 11th Hussars clear the fort at Msus of the Italian rearguard.
3. Combeforce begins marching on 5 February leaving Msus in the morning, hitting the coast road near Sidi Saleh, 10 miles south of Beda Fomm, at 1200hrs.
4. At 1400hrs, a company of 2nd Bn Rifle Brigade is in position across the road with two more companies screening the positions occupied by 4th RHA. Machine-gun and artillery fire brought the Italian column to a halt and the Italians begin to fan out across the desert to the sea to probe south, only to find other elements of the Rifle Brigade astride the road and blocking the way out. At 1430hrs Combeforce finds itself in the path of an entire enemy army (Italian Tenth Army) in retreat.
5. At 1800hrs, the 7th Hussars, supported by elements of 2nd RTR, are ordered to attack the Italians on the road nearer to Beda Fomm at 'The Pimple'.
6. The fighting continues all day on either side of the road, but despite increasing pressure and a growing shortage of ammunition, the Rifle Brigade and 11th Hussars hold out and continue to block the road with sporadic fighting throughout the night of 5/6 February.
7. 6 February, 1045hrs, the Italian 10th Bersaglieri with L-3 light tanks attack the roadblock defended by the 11th Hussars and 2nd Bn Rifle Brigade, but are beaten, with thousands of Italian soldiers surrendering.
8. 6 February, the remainder of 4th Armoured Brigade (7th and 3rd Hussars) arrives and strikes the Italians in their left flank just north of Beda Fomm.
9. 6/7 February, night, quiet prevails in the Beda Fomm area. At 1100hrs on 7 February, General Virginio, Chief of Staff of Italian Tenth Army, arrives at 4th Armored Brigade HQ to surrender.

defenders' attention away to the opposite or east side of the camp with a display of small arms fire and pyrotechnics.

The Matildas crashed through the Italian barbed wire in front of them in the unmined gap, with Italian machine-gun and artillery fire proving ineffective against the tanks' thick armour. Immediately behind them came the motorized infantry of the 2nd Queen's Own Cameron Highlanders, 4th Infantry Division, delivered by Bren carriers. Although the Italian artillerymen fought bravely, their lightly protected sangars and infantry rifle pits were easily neutralized by the British tanks' 2-pdr and machine-gun fire. The attack ended in less than five hours, with over 4,000 Italians taken prisoner. Shortly thereafter, the assault on Tummar West proceeded according to schedule and was secured by the Matildas of 7th RTR and infantry of the 1st Punjab Regiment after two hours of fighting. The 6th Rajputana

Lieutenant-General Henry Maitland 'Jumbo' Wilson, who as GOC, British Troops Egypt (BTE), worked on Operation *Compass* with O'Connor and commanded Wavell's ill-fated expedition to Greece in early 1941. (IWM, E 2008)

General Sir Archibald Wavell, C-in-C Middle East Command, at his desk at GHQ Cairo. Wavell held important meetings with Generals Platt and Cunningham to instruct them on the East African campaign as well as the final meeting with O'Connor and Wilson to launch Operation *Compass*. (IWM, E 451)

Rifles, again with accompanying Matilda tanks, attacked Tummar East, which surrendered in the early morning hours of 10 December. The same morning, the 16th British Infantry Brigade, followed by some late-arriving Matilda tanks and the 11th Indian Infantry Brigade, besieged the port town of Sidi Barrani. The Italians surrendered later that afternoon. By the morning of 11 December, O'Connor's 'limited raid' had netted him a total victory with the prospects looking extremely favourable for even greater conquest. Some 20,000 Italian prisoners with 180 guns and 60 tanks had been taken for the loss of roughly 600 killed.

It was at this juncture that O'Connor learned that the 4th Indian Division was to be transferred to the Sudan for the campaign in East Africa. The relatively untrained 6th Australian Division replaced the 4th Indian Division and under O'Connor, performed superbly, capturing Bardia on 5 January 1941 after a two-day assault. Approximately 38,000 Italian prisoners were captured along with numerous coastal guns, field guns, anti-aircraft artillery pieces and vehicles. Anthony Eden quipped, 'never has so much been surrendered by so many to so few'. On 1 January 1941, the Western Desert Force was renamed XIII Corps.

After Bardia, Wavell set his eyes on Benghazi; however, Churchill was already siphoning off some of XIII Corps and RAF elements for a campaign in Greece. Unfortunately for O'Connor this meant that he would have to compete with Churchill's new Balkan expedition. Owing to the imminence of the German invasion Wavell visited Greece during the second week of January; however, he ordered O'Connor to consider raiding as far west as Benghazi once Tobruk was secured. After the Greeks rejected British troops, in an attempt not to give Hitler a reason to invade, Churchill now moved back from his Aegean plan and urged Wavell to take Benghazi. Tobruk was assaulted by the Australians and fell on 22 January. More than

O'Connor's Attack on Fort Nibeiwa, 9 December 1940

At 0700hrs, heavily armoured Matilda infantry tanks of 7th RTR attacked over an open hardened sand track through the north-west unmined corner of the Italian fortified camp at Nibeiwa without a preparatory direct frontal artillery barrage. From 0300 to 0600hrs, the 4/7th Rajput Regiment masked the move of 7th RTR's assault with small arms and artillery fire from the east and then withdrew. Behind the Matildas (1) came the 2nd Queen's Own Cameron Highlanders (2), who had unloaded from Bren carriers further back. The Matildas and following infantry were to traverse a barbed-wire fence (3) first followed by an uncompleted anti-tank ditch and a masonry wall behind it. Italian infantry and artillery fired back but were overwhelmed by the direct machine-gun and 2-pdr fire from the Matilda tanks, which were impervious to Italian artillery shells. After a two-and-a-half hour mêlée, the British captured Nibeiwa. The 7th RTR lost only two men killed and five wounded while 4,000 Italians were taken prisoner.

Lieutenant-General O'Connor with General Sir Archibald Wavell. Together the two forged Operation *Compass* and shared a penchant for speed, surprise, and secrecy in battle. (IWM, 1549)

25,000 prisoners were taken, along with hundreds of field guns and a score of medium tanks. The second phase of Wavell's offensive was a success.

The battle of Beda Fomm

After capturing Derna on 30 January, O'Connor decided that the Australians could maintain their pursuit of the retreating Italians along the coast. However, his main aim was the total destruction of the Italian Tenth Army. His plan was to have the 7th Armoured Division move swiftly to the south-west in order to cut the road below Benghazi and trap the retreating Italians in the Cyrenaican bulge. Dorman-Smith, who was acting as Wavell's

General Headquarters (GHQ) Cairo, 4 December 1940

To finalize Operation *Compass*, Wavell **(1)** chaired a conference with Lt. Gen. Richard O'Connor, Commanding General, Western Desert Force, **(2)** and Lt. Gen. Sir H. Maitland (Jumbo) Wilson, GOC, British Troops Egypt **(3)**. They examined aerial photographs of the fortified Italian camps of Nibeiwa and the Tummars. Outside of Wavell's office window stands a Marmon Herrington armoured car with a captain of the 1st King's Dragoon Guards beside it. Wavell agreed to plans formulated by his assistant, Brig. Eric Dorman-Smith, to attack through gaps spotted in the minefields on the western sides of the camps, which were to allow Italian supply vehicles to enter. Although these tactics belonged to Dorman-Smith and O'Connor, Wavell's 'fingerprints' were evident: an unorthodox, innovative approach coupled with his twin passions – deception and secrecy.

After adjournment, Wavell gave final approval to Wilson, who issued O'Connor his orders to commence a 'limited five-day raid' on 9 December. Such was Wavell's penchant for secrecy that this was the only written order for Operation *Compass*.

A Matilda tank, which although slow and equipped with only a 2-pdr armament, was heavily armoured (78mm) and thus impervious to Italian anti-tank guns. O'Connor used these tanks extensively throughout Operation *Compass*. (IWM, E 9560)

Soldiers of the 4th Indian Division, which fought brilliantly in the opening phase of Operation *Compass*, prior to their transfer to General Platt for use in his attacks on the Italians in Eritrea during Wavell's highly successful East African campaign. (IWM, E 3660)

liaison officer, returned to Cairo to apprise him of O'Connor's bold new concept. As Dorman-Smith outlined O'Connor's daring scheme, Wavell simply said, 'Tell Dick he can go on and wish him luck from me. He has done well'. Having received Wavell's blessing, O'Connor pressed on with the double envelopment that would become known as the battle of Beda Fomm.

O'Connor held a conference on 31 January and explained how he intended to capture the fleeing Italians along both the coast and in the interior. An ad hoc formation, Combeforce (designated such after its commander, Lt. Col. J. F. B. Combe of the 11th Hussars), left for Msus in the early morning hours of 3 February. This formation consisted of elements of the King's Royal Rifle Corps, Rifle Brigade, Royal Horse Artillery (RHA), 11th Hussars, and King's Dragoon Guards (KDG). Because tanks moved too slowly, Bren carriers were used to transport the infantry of the Rifle Brigade, who hurried after the 11th Hussars under Combe. This force of about 2,000 men was intended to cut the coast road south of Benghazi, and speed was of the essence as the Italians were already starting to pull back from the town. Combeforce occupied Msus on 4 February having travelled over rugged and uncharted terrain, while the 7th Armoured Division arrived a few miles east of Msus on 5 February because of the slower going for tanks.

Combeforce began marching from Msus on 5 February and reached Sidi Saleh on the coast, 10 miles (16km) south of Beda Fomm, at 1200hrs. At 1400hrs, a company from the Rifle Brigade was in position across the road with two more companies screening the positions occupied by the RHA. Machine-gun and artillery fire brought the Italian column to a halt, and they began to fan out across the desert towards the sea to probe south, only to find at 1430hrs other elements of the Rifle Brigade astride the road and blocking the way out. Combeforce found itself in the path of the entire Italian Tenth Army in retreat. At 1800hrs, the 7th Hussars, supported by elements of 2nd RTR were ordered to attack the Italians on the road close to Beda Fomm at 'The Pimple'.

The fighting continued all day on either side of the road, but despite increasing pressure and a growing shortage of ammunition, the Rifle Brigade and 11th Hussars held out and continued to block the road, with sporadic fighting throughout the night of 5/6 February. On 6 February, at 1045hrs, the 10th Italian Bersaglieri with L3 light tanks attacked the roadblock defended by the 11th Hussars and 2nd Rifle Brigade, but were beaten, with thousands of Italian soldiers surrendering. On

Australian infantry near Derna in February 1941, carrying rations and water to the front line. From Derna, O'Connor cut across the Cyrenaican bulge to trap the retreating Italian Tenth Army at Beda Fomm. (IWM, E 1845)

6 February, the remainder of 4th Armoured Brigade (7th and 3rd Hussars) arrived and struck the Italians in their left flank just north of Beda Fomm. The 6th Australian Division had been pressuring the Italians from the east and then the north, so that the Italian force was cramped into a tangled array of vehicles extending 20 miles (32km) in length. Following a relatively peaceful night, at 1100hrs on 7 February, General Virginio, Chief of Staff of Italian Tenth Army, arrived at 4th Armoured Brigade HQ to surrender.

At Beda Fomm, the British completed the destruction of the Italian Tenth Army, capturing an additional 20,000 soldiers along with more than 100 tanks and field guns. In his signal to Wavell, O'Connor, with

A long line of Italian POWs on their way into captivity after surrendering at Beda Fomm in early February 1941. (IWM, E 1380)

The campaign in East Africa

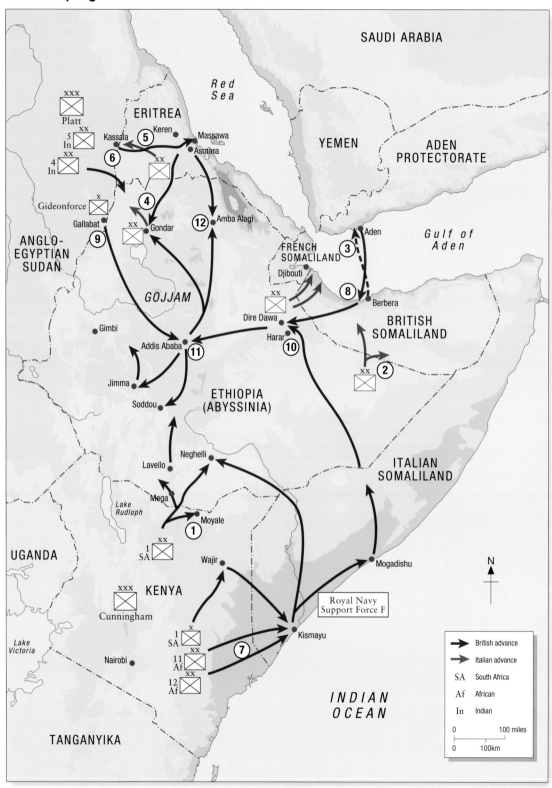

Dorman-Smith's assistance, announced on 7 February 1941, 'Fox killed in the open'. O'Connor modestly noted, 'I think this may be termed a complete victory, as none of the enemy escaped.'

O'Connor thought that after capturing Benghazi, he would receive new orders to press the attack to Tripoli. So Dorman-Smith travelled to Wavell's headquarters in Cairo once again and met with him on 12 February. In Wavell's office, Dorman-Smith found that the maps of the Western Desert no longer hung on the walls, but had been supplanted by maps of Greece and south-eastern Europe. Wavell looked up and told Dorman-Smith, 'You find me busy in my spring campaign', thus, effectively ending any hope of sending XIII Corps further west to Tripoli. In fact, on 10 February, the War Cabinet ruled out any possibility of continuing the advance. Wavell was directed to give first and foremost priority to assisting Greece.

Generals Platt and Cunningham's East African campaigns

Even before the outbreak of war, Wavell had begun to explore ways of removing Italy from power in Abyssinia and in July 1940, Captain Orde Wingate was suggested to lead an Ethiopian insurgency. Wingate, who served in the Sudan Defence Force from 1927 to 1933, had perfected guerrilla tactics as the founder of the Special Night Squads (SNS) in Palestine from 1937 to 1939. It was here that he developed the hit-and-run guerrilla tactics that would serve him well when he led Gideonforce against the Italians in Abyssinia in 1941 (and later the Long Range Penetration Group of Chindits in Operations

1. On 15 July 1940, troops of the 1st South African division recapture Moyale on the Kenya–Ethiopia border.
2. During the months of July and August 1940, Italian troops mass for an invasion of British Somaliland from eastern Ethiopia, which takes place on 4 August.
3. The Italian advance compels the British to evacuate from Berbera to Aden on 19 August.
4. Italian troops from Gondar attack British forces on the Anglo-Sudan border at Kassala on 4 July and at Gallabat on 6 July.
5. An ad hoc force of all-arms British troops, under Colonel Frank Messervy, called Gazelleforce, clashes with and harasses Italian troops along the west-to-east line of Kassala–Asmera in October/November. On 6 November, Brigadier Slim launches his attack with the 10th Indian Brigade to retake Gallabat but is ultimately repelled, with Slim being severely wounded.
6. Platt's 4th Indian Division reoccupies Kassala after the Italians precipitously evacuate it on 18 January 1941. At Wavell's urging, Platt pushes up the start of his assault against Italian fortresses guarding Keren and the route to Asmara (Eritrea's capital) and Massawa, the port on the Red Sea; however, the attack stalls after six days and troops of the 5th Indian Division are transported forward to aid in the resumption of the offensive. Eventually, Keren is assaulted on 15 March and falls on 27 March after ferocious fighting . Asmara falls to Platt on 1 April after the

Italians abandon it. A combined British infantry and tank attack takes Massawa on 8 April, opening the Red Sea.
7. General Cunningham launches his southern sector assault on Italian Somaliland on 11 February 1941 with the 1st South African, 11th African and 12th African divisions, capturing Kismayu three days later. On 25 February, these forces capture Mogadishu with the assistance of the Royal Navy's Support Force F. On 1 March, the Italians begin evacuating Italian Somaliland.
8. The British amphibiously assault Berbera in British Somaliland on 16 March from Aden. Cunningham's South Africans, coming north from Mogadishu, link up with the Aden force on 20 March. This combined force continues their westward advance toward Dire Dawa.
9. Gideonforce enters the Gojjam region with the Patriot insurrection under Wingate in mid-February.
10. Cunningham's forces from the south and British forces from British Somaliland capture Dire Dawa on 28 March.
11. The Ethiopian capital, Addis Ababa, is entered by Gideonforce from the west and Cunningham's forces from the southern sector on 6 April.
12. The Duke of Aosta is compelled to surrender his Italian East African force at Amba Alagi on 19 May, being caught between British northern and southern pincers. Pockets of resistance keep two African divisions occupied until the last Italians surrender on 27 November.

Lieutenant-General
Sir Alan Cunningham, who
commanded the southern
wing of Wavell's pincer
based in Kenya. His forces
conquered Italian
Somaliland and then
swung north into Ethiopia
to help defeat the Duke of
Aosta's forces there, along
with General Platt's
northern wing and
Major Orde Wingate's
Gideonforce.
(IWM, E 6661)

Longcloth and *Thursday* against the Japanese in Burma in 1943 and 1944).

Another Wavell protégé, Tony Simonds, was also vital to the Ethiopian campaign. In 1937, Simonds was serving on Wavell's Intelligence Staff in Palestine where he worked closely with Wingate, providing information and targets for the SNS. He was also one of the few officers who could coexist with Wingate. When Wavell became GOC-in-Chief, Middle East Command, Simonds and Wingate worked together again, as Gideonforce in the autumn of 1940 preparing an invasion of Abyssinia from Khartoum. Simonds also operated independently, organizing Mission 101 on Wingate's left wing. He had some startling successes, bluffing his way past superior Italian forces who were bewildered by his hit-and-run tactics and ingenuity. After Abyssinia, Simonds was recalled to Cairo where he ran N Section of Dudley Clarke's A Force.

On 2 December 1940, Wavell presided over a meeting in Cairo with Platt and Cunningham. Wavell told Platt at this meeting that the 4th Indian Division (now under O'Connor) would begin to move to the Sudan about the middle of December in order to attack the Duke of Aosta's Italian forces in Ethiopia. Wavell initially directed Platt to recapture Kassala on the border of the Sudan and Eritrea by March 1941. However, when the Italians abandoned Kassala in January 1941, Wavell ordered Platt to pursue the Italians vigorously into Eritrea. Wavell also continued to pressurize the Italians in the Gallabat area on the Sudan–Ethiopia border, hoping to foment an insurrection among the Ethiopian population. In Kenya to the south, Cunningham was to advance to the Ethiopian frontier to the north and Italian Somaliland to the east. On 1 February, Wavell informed Dill that he had given instructions 'to both Platt and Cunningham for maximum effort they can make against Italian East Africa during the next two months as an expedition to Greece was looming'.

In January 1941, following the Italian withdrawal from Kassala, the Ethiopian Emperor Haile Selassie had moved across the Sudanese frontier into Ethiopia, with Orde Wingate commanding the Patriot forces in the Gojjam region of western Ethiopia. By mid-February, Platt's 4th Indian Division was in position to attack the Italian fortresses around the town of Keren, where the bulk of the Italian forces were located. Platt reinforced the 4th Indian Division with the 5th Indian Division, but a further assault on Keren on 15 March ended in stalemate. Wavell himself visited Platt at Keren on 25 March to help with the tactical planning. Wavell wrote, 'As soon as I had a good look at the position, I said to Platt that it looked to me as if the way through was straight up the main road, neglecting the high peaks to north and south'. The suggestion was implemented and the attack succeeded, with Keren falling to the British on 27 March. The victory at Keren enabled Wavell to continue to juggle his forces strategically from one corner of his theatre to another, with the 4th Indian Division being rapidly redeployed to North Africa. After Keren, the Italians abandoned Asmara on 1 April, while a combined infantry and tank assault by Platt on the position at Massawa resulted in its surrender on 8 April. Eritrea was now cleared of the Italians and the threat to Allied shipping in the Red Sea was removed. This coincided with the fall of Addis Ababa to the British on 6 April 1941.

An RAF armoured car campaigning in Iraq in May 1941. Wavell had to improvise and form ad hoc units in Palestine, which travelled great distances to suppress the Iraqi rebellion. (IWM, E 2943E)

To the south, Cunningham had sent the 11th and 12th East African Divisions against Kismayu in Italian Somaliland with the support of the Royal Navy (Force F) on 11 February 1941. The 12th African Division entered the city after a brief but fierce struggle on 14 February and Cunningham next assaulted Mogadishu, which fell to his forces on 25 February.

Following Keren's surrender in the north, the Duke of Aosta focused his remaining forces on Amba Alagi. In a pincer movement, the 5th Indian Division assaulted Amba Alagi from the north on 4 May, while Cunningham's troops attacked from the south on 10 May, completing the encirclement of the Italian fortress. Fearing for the safety of his wounded men, the Duke of Aosta began negotiations for a truce on 16 May, and he finally surrendered his garrison on 19 May. This ended the major fighting in the East African campaign, though some Italian garrisons held out till November.

The strategic vision behind the East Africa campaign belonged to Wavell. As he wrote himself, 'the ultimate pattern of the conquest was a pincer movement on the largest scale, through Eritrea and Somaliland converging on Amba Alagi, combined with a direct thrust through Western Abyssinia by the Patriot forces... this result was not foreseen in the original plan but arose gradually through the development of events'. Wavell conquered Italian East Africa through shifting his forces on simultaneous fronts in a fashion resembling the Confederate general Robert E. Lee's victory over the more numerous Army of the Potomac at Chancellorsville in May 1863. Although halted in Cyrenaica, at this point Wavell revealed his tenacity by continuing his East African campaign rather than withdrawing Cunningham's units and Platt's remaining forces for either the Libyan fighting or the expedition to Greece.

Campaigning on five fronts

From April to June 1941, Wavell fought the Axis powers or their proxies on five different fronts. Despite his two enormous victories in North and East Africa, Wavell was a reluctant combatant, but nonetheless the ultimate victor over a German-sponsored Arab revolt in Iraq (April/May 1941) and a winner over Vichy French forces in Syria (June/July 1941). Wavell's ambivalence towards these missions centred on the twin threats posed by the developing debacles in Greece and Crete in April and May, and Rommel's conquest of Cyrenaica and siege of Tobruk, which resulted in the subsequent British failed attacks at Halfaya Pass and Fort Capuzzo on the Libyan–Egyptian frontier, Operation *Brevity* (15 May) and Operation *Battleaxe* on 15–17 June. These defeats provoked Wavell's replacement by Auchinleck as C-in-C, Middle East Command.

Victories in Iraq and Syria

Iraq had been a British mandate from 1920 until it acquired independence in 1932, following which the two countries signed a mutual assistance pact. Simply put, Britain was prepared to defend Iraq to keep the oil flowing. In 1941, the Empire received all of its oil from Iraq except for Lend-Lease stocks from American sources. If Iraqi oil fell into German hands, coupled with an interruption in the transatlantic flow from the United States, Britain would probably have had to surrender.

Iraq's loss would also have fanned the flames of Arab nationalism, most notably in Egypt and Palestine, which could have made the Middle East indefensible. The loss of the Suez Canal to Rommel, together with a successful rebellion in Iraq, would have threatened British control over India. Thus British control over Iraq was vital.

Britain maintained two RAF bases in Iraq. The larger one was located at Habbaniya on the Euphrates River about 50 miles (80km) to the west of Baghdad. Another RAF base was situated at Shaibah, approximately 15 miles (24km) south of the port of Basra. Britain also maintained a Military Mission to Iraq, and had the right to move military forces throughout the country. At the outset of the rebellion, Iraq was ruled by the pro-British Emir Abdullah. However, a number of Arab nationalists including the Grand Mufti of Jerusalem, who had connections with and support from Nazi

1. First contingent of the 10th Indian Division disembarks (uninvited) at Basra on 19 April 1941 after coming from India. Remainder of 20th Indian Infantry Brigade arrives at Basra on 29 April to support the Shaibah RAF base there.
2. Rashid Ali's troops surround the RAF station at Habbaniya, 50 miles west of Baghdad on 29 April.
3. 2 May, British Wellington bombers attack the Iraqis besieging Habbaniya, who in turn begin artillery shelling of the RAF garrison there.
4. Maj. Gen. J. G. W. Clarke, commanding 1st Cavalry Division in Palestine, organizes Kingcol, a column under the command of Brig. J. J. Kingstone (4th Cavalry Brigade), which is to serve as the vanguard of his Habforce to relieve Habbaniya. Kingcol begins moving on 11 May.
5. 14 May, Kingcol is augmented by the Arab Legion under the command of Major John Bagot Glubb (Glubb Pasha).
6. Siege of Habbaniya suddenly lifted on 6 May after besieging Iraqi troops inexplicably flee. Kingcol reaches Habbaniya on 18 May after being strafed for three days by German aircraft, and prepares for attack on Falluja.

7. Elements of the 10th Indian Division continue to pacify the Basra vicinity. Flooding and lack of transport hamper their north-westward movement for weeks. 21st Indian Infantry Brigade arrives in Basra on 6 May to protect the city and port facilities.
8. Habforce arrives at Habbaniya on 25 May and reaches the outskirts of Baghdad, fighting breaks out on 28 May. Rashid Ali and the Grand Mufti flee to Iran on 30 May after Iraqi troops are defeated by Habforce. Baghdad surrenders on 31 May.
9. Slim's 10th Indian Division troops move north on 10 June to open up communications between Basra and Habbaniya. All vestiges of pro-Axis forces are eliminated by 18 June.
10. Habforce and elements of the 10th Indian Division, fresh from their fighting in Iraq, march westwards on 23 June towards Homs and Aleppo to attack the Vichy forces tenaciously fighting other British, Australian and Free French contingents from Palestine.
11. Palmyra surrenders to Habforce on 3 July 1941. Habforce and 10th Indian Division continue fighting the Vichy French until 12 July.

Wavell's operation in Iraq

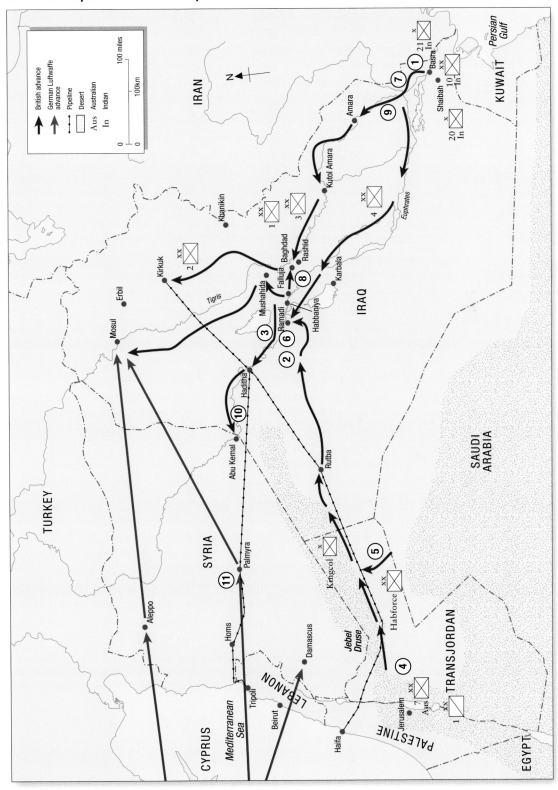

Germany and was granted asylum in Iraq after expulsion from Palestine for his part in the Arab Rebellion there, wanted to foment insurrection and undermine Abdullah's authority in order to weaken Britain's dominance over the country. Additionally, a number of Iraqi Army colonels, eager to expel the British, received support from the Nazi Ambassador to Iraq. This military cabal acquired French weapons from arsenals in Syria, smuggled into Iraq by German agents. On 1 April 1941 the Anglophobe Rashid Ali el Ghailani led a *coup d'état* that overthrew Abdullah and on 2 May laid siege to the RAF base at Habbaniya, provoking a British intervention.

On 18 April, a brigade group from India Command landed to secure Basra. At Wavell's suggestion, General Auchinleck, C-in-C, India Command, initially bore the military responsibility for Iraq and he offered to move up to two divisions to this hotspot. Owing to his commitments in Cyrenaica, Greece, Crete and Italian East Africa, Wavell was reluctant to have Middle East Command become embroiled in an Iraqi uprising. However, Churchill was adamant that Wavell ensure Basra's security, Habbaniya's relief and the maintenance of land communication through Iraq to Turkey. Auchinleck landed two additional brigades from India at Basra in early May, but on 2 May the War Cabinet told Wavell that Iraq was now under his sphere of military control as C-in-C, Middle East Command. Despite his objections, Wavell was compelled to dispatch a motorized brigade from Palestine to Iraq. Ironically, the Habbaniya garrison, reinforced by RAF aircraft, lifted its own siege before the brigade, designated 'Habforce', left Palestine.

On 23 May, as the battle for Crete raged, Wavell arrived in Basra to discuss plans with Auchinleck. There, he ordered Habforce to advance onto Baghdad, which was reached on 30 May, causing Rashid Ali and his confederates to seek asylum in Iran.

Following the collapse of France in June 1940, Syria remained under the control of a Vichy regime that was clearly pro-Nazi both in metropolitan France and her African and Middle Eastern colonies. German agents were working hard from Syria to provoke and maintain rebellions across the Middle East and, on 5 May, the Vichy authorities and the Nazis agreed to send French war material from Syria to Iraq and allow German aircraft to use Syrian airfields to attack British bases there.

At the end of April, London instructed Wavell to be prepared to send a force in support of possible French resistance in Syria. Furthermore, General Charles de Gaulle was eager to intervene in Syria using his Free French forces. After the capture of Massawa in East Africa by Platt in early April, Wavell concentrated all Free French units serving in the Middle East in Egypt. Responding to de Gaulle's requests, Wavell redesignated these Free French forces as a division and stationed them in Palestine just in case they should be needed in Syria.

When action was demanded against Syria, Wavell had two options. First, he could send the Free French force on its own into Syria to combat the Vichy forces and any Germans there. Second, he could transfer troops from the Western Desert for the Syrian operation. His instructions from London were irritatingly vague; to 'create as large a force as possible without detriment to the Western Desert'. Furthermore, Churchill weighed in with his requirement that the Syrian campaign was not to weaken the defence of Crete.

Despite urging from de Gaulle, Wavell refused to allow a solo Free French operation. He realized he had to act decisively as if the Luftwaffe became entrenched in Syria then Egypt, the Canal Zone and Cyprus would all be in range of their aircraft. Thus he ordered most of the 7th Australian Division into northern Palestine along with a brigade from the 4th Indian Division, which was returning to Egypt from Eritrea. He added the mobile elements of the 1st Cavalry Division, already in Palestine, to the Free French battalions to comprise an ad hoc assault force. In his own dispatch, Wavell wrote, 'As usual, one of the principal difficulties was to find the necessary transport and signals for the force and the usual process of scraping from other units and formations had to be resorted to produce any force at all'. On 8 June the assault on Syria began, at the same time as the surrender and evacuation of Crete and the preparations for *Battleaxe*, Wavell's final operation against Rommel.

General Wilson assumed local command of the Syrian campaign and launched his attack from Palestine and Transjordan. Damascus fell on 21 June and Wilson turned his advance on to Beirut in Lebanon. Wavell now redirected Habforce from Iraq across the Syrian Desert to attack Palmyra and Homs, while the 10th Indian Division moved against Aleppo. These additional forces, plus the addition of aircraft no longer needed for *Battleaxe*, broke the back of Vichy resistance and Syria came under British control on 11 July, within days of Wavell leaving the Middle East Command for India.

Setbacks in Greece and Crete

Wavell's expedition to Greece in March/April 1941 and the defence of Crete in late May were at face value outright disasters. While O'Connor was winning his staggering victory at Beda Fomm in early February 1941, the situation in the Balkans was deteriorating. Greece sought British air and naval assistance, but given the situation at home, London decided that any support had to come from Wavell's Middle East Command. With the Italian threat to Egypt and Cyrenaica eliminated, the Defence Council prioritized Greece over the Western Desert.

The strategy that Wavell suggested was the withdrawal of the entire Greek battle-line to a more compact front, to create a counterattacking reserve force. However, the Greek commander, General Papagos, disagreed with Wavell's approach. On 6 April the Germans launched a broad assault throughout the Balkans. Wavell had committed the New Zealand Division under Maj. Gen. Bernard Freyberg to the Aliakmon Line under the overall command of General Wilson (W Force). The British 1st Armoured Brigade was on the Salonika plain and the 6th Australian Division had just landed. Most of Greece's divisions were on the Albanian front, holding off the Italian invasion. Within days, the Greek line crumbled, forcing Wilson to withdraw the armoured brigade. The Aliakmon Line was outflanked and

The defence of Crete, 20–31 May 1941

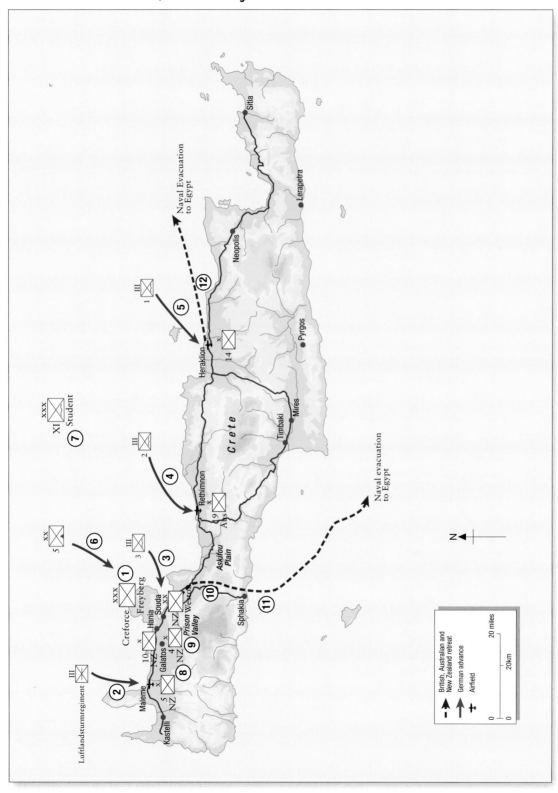

the British retreat began on the night of 11/12 April. Wavell visited the Greek front to confer with Wilson and the Australian I Corps commander, Thomas Blamey. However, within days of this meeting Wavell realized that the troops would need to be withdrawn, and the Royal Navy began to draw up its plans for evacuation. On 17 April, Churchill gave Wavell permission to withdraw Wilson's Commonwealth forces from Greece, with Wavell promising to hold Crete.

The Allied evacuation ended on 30 April, with approximately 25,000 troops being evacuated to Crete. Here Freyberg was appointed by Wavell to command the garrison, since Wilson was evacuated to Jerusalem to command the Baghdad relief mission. Around another 16,000 men were taken straight to Egypt by the Royal Navy. Many troops were trapped in the Peloponnese and taken prisoner, while every major piece of equipment was lost. The following day the Luftwaffe started its bombardment of Crete. Wavell himself thought that the 'expedition to Greece was ill-starred from the first.... The German attack took place while the Imperial forces were still in process of concentration and before it had time to get properly settled down.... Thus, while the whole expedition was something in the nature of a gamble, the dice were loaded against it from the first. It was not really such a forlorn hope from the military point of view as it may seem from its results.'

The German invasion of Crete, codenamed Operation *Merkur*, was the only operation during the war in which an extensive strategic target was

1. About 25,000 Allied troops are evacuated from Greece to Crete. Wavell appoints New Zealander Maj. Gen. Bernard Freyberg, to command Creforce on 30 April 1941.

2. 20 May, 0800hrs, glider-borne troops of the Luftlandsturmregiment, commanded by Generalmajor E. Meindl, and ad hoc groups of *Fallschirmjäger* arrive at Maleme, attempting to capture the airfield there. Maleme is defended by the 5th New Zealand Brigade under the command of Brig. J. Hargest.

3. 20 May, 0815hrs, Fallschirmjägerregiment 3 parachutes into 'Prison Valley' to the west of Hania and Souda. The German paratroops meet strong resistance from the 4th and 10th New Zealand Brigades.

4. 20 May, 1615hrs, Fallschirmjägerregiment 2 parachutes into the area east of Rethimnon in an attempt to capture the airfield there, defended by the 19th Australian Brigade.

5. 20 May, 1730hrs, Fallschirmjägerregiment 1 airdrops around the airfield at Heraklion, defended by the British 14th Infantry Brigade. At nightfall on 20 May, only part of Maleme was held by the German paratroops. None of Freyberg's airfields had been captured at the end of fighting on 20–21 May.

6. 21 May, the Royal Navy intercepted a convoy of ships transferring elements of 5. Gebirgsjäger-Division and essentially destroys III/Gebirgsjäger-Regiment 100 at sea, though at considerable loss to the British fleet. After this foray, the Luftwaffe controls the skies over the sea lanes during daylight.

7. Generalmajor Kurt Student, commander of Fliegerkorps XI, continues to fly in reinforcements on 23 May with only Maleme in German control, despite a failed Allied counterattack to drive the Germans from the airfield on 21–22 May. The other three air-landing sites are still in Allied control since the German paratroops are unable to break through Freyberg's defensive lines.

8. 24–26 May, heavily reinforced German forces continue to drive eastwards from the captured airfield at Maleme to threaten Hania. 25 May, a large German force breaks through the defensive line and captures Galatos. Freyberg's forces attempt to form a new defence line to the west of Hania on 26 May.

9. 27 May, the Germans deploy a five-regiment attack against Freyberg's 'Force Reserve' (consisting of Royal Welch Fusiliers, Northumberland Hussars and the 1st Ranger Bn). After being surrounded by the Germans, some of the 'Force Reserve' breaks out to rejoin the main force at Souda. The Allies mount a counterattack with elements of the 19th Australian and 5th New Zealand Brigades, which keeps an evacuation route to Sphakia open and buys time for an Allied withdrawal to get started. On 27 May, Wavell advises London that he had already ordered the evacuation from Crete to proceed.

10. 28–30 May, the Allies begin their fighting retreat from the east of Souda over the mountain road to Sphakia.

11. Freyberg's troops (17,000) are evacuated from Sphakia to Alexandria by the Royal Navy on 29–31 May. The rearguard consists of New Zealanders, Australians and Royal Marines.

12. On the morning of 28 May, Allied battalion commanders around Heraklion are informed that a Royal Navy squadron will evacuate them that night. By 0245hrs on 29 May, about 3,500 men set sail for Alexandria. On 1 June the remaining Allied troops were ordered to surrender at 0900hrs.

attacked and secured by airborne assault. Before the Greek expedition, Britain had used Crete as a naval refuelling base, and had reserved the option of turning the island into a fortress based on the airfields at Heraklion, Maleme and Retimo. However, Wavell was aware that all of the island's strategic points lay on the north coast. The lack of landing facilities on the south coast, and no road across the island by which reinforcements and supplies from Egypt could have been sent to the north coast, seriously hampered the defence. Wavell wrote in his despatch, 'it had always been intended to develop landing places on the south of the island and roads from them to the north, in order to avoid the exposed passage round the north of the island; but there had never been sufficient means to carry this out'. The only factor that seemed to favour Wavell's position on Crete after the evacuation from Greece was the underestimation of his strength by the Germans, who thought that there were only 5,000 British troops on the island. Freyberg's defence of Crete was based on preventing a hostile seizure of the airfields and the New Zealanders' strongpoints were based at Maleme, Retimo, Heraklion and Suda Bay. Unfortunately, with limited transport on the island each of the four defence sectors would be independent of the others and they could not mutually support each other. Wavell later wrote, 'He [Freyberg] did not anticipate, any more than anyone else, the overwhelming strength in which the German Air Force was to make the attack, nor how carefully and skilfully their plans had been laid nor the losses they were prepared to accept to attain their object.'

On 20 May, heavy bombing of Heraklion and Maleme preceded the landing of parachute and glider troops around Maleme (0800hrs) and Heraklion (1730hrs). By nightfall on the first day of the battle the four major defence zones remained in Freyberg's control, with the German paratroops only established in force at Maleme. The German High Command had

Wavell inspecting the garrison at Suda Bay on Crete in November 1940. The northern coast of Crete was attacked by the Luftwaffe's paratroops and air-landing glider-borne troops in late May 1941. After days of furious fighting British and Commonwealth troops under Maj. Gen. Freyberg had to be evacuated by the Royal Navy. (IWM, E 1179)

planned to overcome all resistance in three days. The next day, after the withdrawal of some New Zealand troops, Heraklion and Maleme airfields were attacked again. An Allied counterattack on Maleme on 22 May, although it reached the eastern edge of Maleme airfield, was forced to withdraw, leaving this landing ground in German hands. Heraklion still remained under Allied control. On 23 May, German airborne assaults continued and the Allied troops commenced a withdrawal to a new line near Galatos. The following day the British front lines at Galatos came under attack by elements of *Gebirgsjäger* regiments. Continued fighting along the Galatos front raged on 25 May until the eventual collapse of the British defence line, and withdrawal to Suda Bay began on 26 May. Further troops withdrew to Sphakion to be taken off by sea. By the end of the seventh day, Freyberg signalled Wavell that his force had reached the limits of their endurance. So on 27 May, Wavell told Churchill that Crete was no longer defensible and London ordered the island's evacuation, which occurred in an orderly fashion from 28 May until 1 June. Through the efforts of the Mediterranean Fleet, 16,000 men were brought off the Cretan beaches and harbours to Egypt. A tremendous feat given the dominance of the Luftwaffe, and only the fastest warships were able to patrol off the north coast of Crete and even then only at night.

Wavell wrote to the evacuees, 'I thank you for the great courage and endurance with which you attempted the defence of the island of Crete. I am well aware of the difficulties under which you carried out your task and that it must have appeared to many of you that you had been asked to do the impossible, and that you were insufficiently equipped and supported. As Commander-in-Chief I accept the responsibility for what was done. It was for strategical reasons necessary to hold the island of Crete if this could reasonably be done.'

Rommel's conquest of Cyrenaica

In early 1941, Hitler's original plan to bolster the Italians after the defeat at Beda Fomm was to provide German anti-tank, anti-aircraft and armoured units. Initially, a motorized light division (5. leichte-Division) and the 15. Panzer-Division were ordered to Libya on 20 March. Generalleutnant Erwin Rommel, aged 49, was appointed the commander of this force. Rommel studied Wavell's successes in Operation *Compass* and learned wisely. On 12 February, Rommel arrived in Tripoli and exceeded his orders by assuming control of the German forward area and ordering his newly arriving armoured units east towards the British. Rather than waiting for reinforcements, he pushed his reconnaissance units forward to bluff the British into believing he had superior strength. In fact, Wavell was not only up against superior German numbers, but, for the first time in the desert war, the British commander had inferior armour and anti-tank weapons. On 31 March, Rommel attacked and captured the British defensive position at Mersa Brega.

After seeing the British retreat, Rommel drove forward without orders to Agedabia. Wavell left Cairo for the desert and, in order to stem Rommel's advance, he ordered O'Connor to leave Cairo to join General Neame, the British commander in Cyrenaica, as an advisor. Rommel's intent was to cut the Cyrenaica bulge, the reverse of what O'Connor had achieved only weeks

1. 5 March, at Wingate's 3rd Indian Division (Special Force) HQ at Lalaghat in India, a hastily arranged photoreconnaissance reveals teak logs stretched across the proposed Chindit air-landing field, 'Piccadilly'. After a meeting, Wingate and his 77th Brigade commander, Brigadier Calvert, agreed that the glider landings scheduled for later that night should be diverted to another landing field, 'Broadway'. After Broadway is secured, engineers are to arrive to create airstrips and convert it into a Wingate-styled stronghold.

2. A second operation begins that same night to fly the advance guard of 111th Brigade into 'Chowringhee', a landing zone some 50 miles south-west of Broadway between the Shweli and Irrawaddy rivers. This brigade is also originally intended to fly into Piccadilly, but with Calvert's men now diverted to Broadway, the 111th Brigade now has to land at Chowringhee from where it will cross the Irrawaddy to march north to rendezvous with two of the other battalions landing at Broadway.

3. 16th Brigade under Brigadier Fergusson is the only Special Force brigade to march into Burma. The start point for their trek is the Ledo Road with their destination being the Indaw area. Fergusson's 16th Brigade starts its march on 5 February and crosses the Chindwin on 1 March. The 111th Brigade is to provide assistance for 16th Brigade once it arrived in the Indaw area to set up a stronghold, 'Aberdeen', which it would garrison and from which it woudl patrol for six weeks against the Japanese at Indaw.

4. Calvert takes five columns of 77th Brigade from Broadway and clashes with IJA forces at Henu on 16/17 March. After a hand-to-hand mêlée, the Chindits secure the area and began to fortify what is to become the 'White City' stronghold. The

Japanese launch their numerous counterattacks against White City, beginning on 21 March.

5. Calvert's Chindits sortie out of White City to attack the Japanese around Mawlu and destroys two battalions and engineer companies from the IJA 18th Division.

6. 1 April, the Japanese 24th Independent Mixed Brigade, reinforced to division size, establishes its base in the Sepein–Mawlu area and launches a full-scale attack on White City on 6 April. On 17 April, the Japanese make their last assault on this stronghold.

7. Early May, 111th Brigade establishes a new stronghold, 'Blackpool', in the Hopin–Mogaung area and is immediately attacked before a strong defensive perimeter can be constructed. 77th Brigade leaves White City to support the eastern side of Blackpool against Japanese attacks from Mogaung.

8. Evacuation of White City by 14th Brigade commences on 9/10 May as the theatre of Chindit operations continues to shift north to assist Stilwell's offensive towards Myitkyina and Mogaung. Broadway and Aberdeen are also abandoned.

9. 3rd West African Brigade marches north to support the 14 Brigade on the western side of Blackpool. Maj. Gen. Lentaigne, who takes over following Wingate's death, knows that for Blackpool to hold out it needs the support of his other brigades to combat increasing IJA troop strength in the area.

10. 20 May, the IJA 53rd Division arrives in the Hopin area and starts its attacks on Blackpool.

11. 25 May, the remnants of the 111th Brigade evacuate Blackpool under intense Japanese pressure.

12. IJA 33rd, 15th, and 31st Divisions attack Imphal and Kohima during the ill-fated *U-Go* advance into India.

Wingate's Operation *Thursday*, March–August 1944

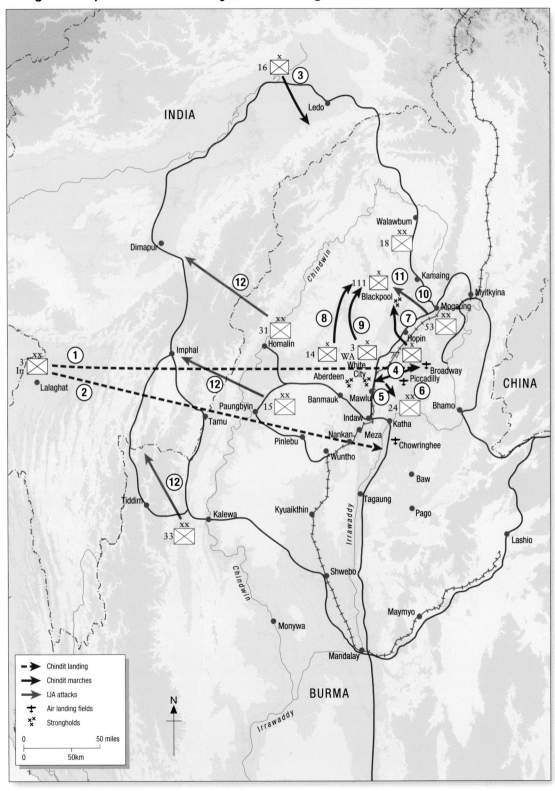

INDIA

16 x 3

Ledo

Dimapur

Walawbum

18 xx

Kamaing

Chindwin

111 x
Blackpool

10

Myitkyina

11

31 xx
Homalin

Mogaung

53 xx

Imphal

14 x
3
WA
White
City

Aberdeen

x

Hopin

x xx

7

4

Broadway

CHINA

Paungbyin

15 xx
Banmauk

Mawlu

Piccadilly

6

5

24 xx

Bhamo

Tamu

Pinlebu

Nankan

Indaw

Katha

Meza

Chowringhee

Wuntho

Tiddim

12

Kalewa

Kyuaikthin

Tagaung

Baw

Pago

33 xx

Irrawaddy

Lashio

Shwebo

Monywa

Maymyo

Mandalay

BURMA

Chindwin

Irrawaddy

➤ ➤ ➤	Chindit landing
➤	Chindit marches
➤	IJA attacks
✝	Air landing fields
xx xx	Strongholds

N

0   50 miles

0   50km

41

before; his first objective was Derna and then Tobruk. Sending other detachments along the coast road, Rommel's forces entered Benghazi on 4 April. It was at this juncture that Neame ordered a general withdrawal.

Beginning on 6 April, the 9th Australian Division withdrew from Derna into Tobruk. Wavell reacted to Rommel's attack and the disintegration of his forces in Cyrenaica by recognizing that Tobruk was the linchpin in the region. He had to keep the port and its facilities, the water, the arsenal and its fuel out of Rommel's hands. Tobruk was reinforced with a brigade from the 7th Australian Division, while the other brigades were sent to O'Connor's Egyptian defences at Mersa Matruh. Wavell proved his mettle here as a strategist, tactician, quartermaster and director at a troop depot making sure that everything available was sent to reinforce Tobruk, while also keeping some reserves at hand in Egypt. Wavell was determined to hold Tobruk as a fortress while also maintaining the frontier at Sollum as a threat to Rommel as he invested Tobruk. At this critical hour, it was Wavell's decision to defend both the Tobruk and Sollum positions strongly in order to strangle Rommel's offensive, so that Egypt and the Nile Delta were protected, even as the Greek expedition was becoming a fiasco.

During the early hours of 7 April, Generals O'Connor and Neame were both captured by the Germans as they tried to get back to the British lines. Wavell received this news late on the day of their capture and flew the following day to Tobruk to lend his personal support to the junior officers as the situation deteriorated.

Wavell's last offensive against Rommel

On 1 May, as Rommel attacked Tobruk, Wavell began to plan an offensive, Operation *Battleaxe*, once armoured reinforcements, the 'Tiger' convoy, arrived later in the month. However, before the new tanks were even off-loaded Wavell acted on intelligence received, which revealed that Rommel had limited armour along the Egyptian frontier. So he struck at the Germans by sending all of the remaining British armour in the Western Desert along with the Support Group of 7th Armoured Division to attack on 15 May in Operation *Brevity*. The German positions at Halfaya Pass, Capuzzo and Sollum were captured by the British. However, fierce German counterattacks by elements of 5. leichte-Division and 15. Panzer-Division recaptured Capuzzo and Sollum. Halfaya Pass remained in British possession until 26–27 May, when Rommel attacked and retook this key location. Halfaya Pass was vital since it was the only route for British vehicles and armour to go up the desert escarpment and across to Cyrenaica. By the end of May, 15. Panzer-Division had deployed some 160 tanks along the Egyptian frontier, of which Wavell was completely unaware.

At this point, Crete was still occupied, the Iraqi Revolt and Ethiopian campaign were still ongoing, while the situation in Syria was alarming. Wavell was also concerned about the advantages held by the German armour, cabling Dill on the 28th to note that the quality of British armour as compared with that possessed by his German counterpart did not enable him to give battle with complete confidence. Wavell kept delaying the start of his offensive until 15 June. From the attack's outset, the plan went awry. A coastal column of British armour was not able to recapture either Sollum or Halfaya Pass. Another British central column took Capuzzo again, but it too failed to dislodge the enemy from Halfaya Pass. As the attacks proceeded, numerous British tanks were lost. Over the next two days, Rommel was intercepting British wireless traffic and redirected his Panzers skilfully to prevent the British armour from carrying out its plans. Wavell had flown up to the battlefield but clearly saw the futility of his position. On 17 June, the British force returned to Sidi Barrani, while Wavell withdrew the 7th Armoured Division to Mersa Matruh to refit, leaving mobile reconnaissance forces to keep Rommel at bay. The British lost over 150 tanks. Wavell wrote, 'Had [our] tank crews had more practice with their weapons they would have destroyed a much larger number of enemy tanks; and had they all been more experienced in maintenance there would have been fewer tanks out of action through mechanical breakdown; so that instead of being outnumbered at the end of the battle, we should have been in sufficient strength to have defeated the enemy.' Unfortunately in the Prime Minister's eyes his newly reinforced armoured force had been decimated convincingly by Rommel's DAK.

Commander-in-Chief, India

After Wavell received his telegram of dismissal on 22 June 1941, Dill had wanted to bring him back to England to rest but Churchill vetoed his CIGS. The Prime Minister ordered him directly to India to exchange places with Auchinleck. As he did in the Middle East, he requested more resources and asked for the inclusion of Burma within his sphere of command, which he

Wavell inspecting the 8th Gurkhas along with Auchinleck, who replaced him in the Middle East Theatre. (IWM, IND 4977)

Wavell as C-in-C, India, inspecting soldiers of the 2nd Gordon Highlanders in Singapore in November 1941, during the last month of peace in the Far East. (IWM, FE 375)

General Wavell (second from left) and General Alexander (left) with Chinese officers in Burma. The British suffered a humiliating defeat at the hands of the Japanese there in 1942.
(IWM, IND 859)

obtained after the Japanese attacked in December 1941. Once again, the breadth of Wavell's command was enormous and included India, Burma, Malaya and dealings with China.

After Japan's entry into the war, Wavell was given a new responsibility, the ABDA (American, British, Dutch, and Australian) command, which came into being on 3 January 1942. This command was ludicrous since it encompassed all Allied forces in Burma, Singapore, Malaya, the Dutch East Indies, the Philippines (of which Wavell never assumed control) and North-West Australia. However, General George Marshall, the US Army Chief of Staff, had the operational goal of one single supreme commander in each theatre of war. In order to win over a reluctant Churchill to his concept of command structure, Marshall suggested Wavell as supreme commander for the whole of the Far East theatre. Under the ABDA command, Wavell, the C-in-C India, set up his headquarters at Lembang in Java on 15 January 1942 in order to oversee all Allied forces in the Far East, taking his orders directly from the Combined Chiefs of Staff in Washington. Fortunately, the onerous ABDA command was disbanded on 22 February 1942 as by that time Hong Kong, Singapore, Malaya, the Dutch East Indies and other possessions were already lost. General Sir Alan Brooke, the new CIGS, thought 'the whole scheme wild and half-baked' with Wavell himself noting that it was a 'pretty tall order… I had been handed not just the baby but quadruplets'. Even Churchill knew that 'it was almost certain that he would have to bear a load of defeat in a scene of confusion'.

The list of military disasters that the Japanese imposed at will on the Allies was extensive. Wavell was neither able to stave off defeat nor to generate victory. Even personal visits to Singapore a week before its fall or to Burma in early March or the hastening of Lt. Gen. Harold Alexander to command

Chindits during Operation *Longcloth* set demolition charges to destroy a railway bridge on the north–south Mandalay–Myitkyina railway. (IWM, SE 7921)

Major-General Orde Wingate, second from right, examines last-minute reconnaissance photographs with his British subordinates and American Air Commando officers just prior to the start of Operation *Thursday*. (IWM, MH 7884)

the British ground forces in Burma failed to help stem the Japanese tide. Wavell's offensive into the Arakan by the 14th Indian Division between December 1942 and May 1943 was also incapable of breaking through the newly fortified Japanese defensive positions there.

Wavell continued, though, to turn to unorthodox strategy and tactics. Most prominent among many schemes was the summoning of Orde Wingate to India. Wavell personally authorized the first Chindit expedition, Operation *Longcloth,* which began on 8 February 1943. The value of Wingate's long-range penetration operations has remained controversial, but this first Chindit expedition certainly proved that British troops could fight the Japanese in the jungle. The positive propaganda derived and the favourable impression made on Churchill by Operation *Longcloth* helped offset the damage done by the failure in the Arakan. As noted by Louis Allen, the British Army after the defeats of 1942 in the Far East, 'needed an immense uplifting of spirit. It needed Orde Wingate… devotees of the dull and staid will decry his flamboyance, histrionic procedures, and the publicity which attended them. They miss the point. What the press and world opinion made of Wingate's initial exploits, infused a new spirit into the affairs of Burma.'

An RAF transport parachuting supplies to Chindit columns and strongholds in Burma during Operation *Thursday*.
(IWM, KY 471207)

Wingate and his American Air Commando colleagues provided new tactics in addition to élan. They pioneered jungle airborne assault and resupply. As an example, Brigadier Calvert led 77th Indian Infantry Brigade as glider-borne infantry into the Burmese landing field called 'Broadway' on 5/6 March 1944 to commence Operation *Thursday*. Calvert then marched five Chindit

A Dakota transport aircraft, flown by both American and British crews, resupplied the Chindits and brought in heavy armaments to fortify Wingate's strongholds, such as White City. (IWM, IND 5277)

columns towards Mawlu, a Japanese railhead supplying Imperial Japanese Army (IJA) troops in Northern Burma. On 16 March, a furious hand-to-hand combat engagement took place at a small village, Henu, which had been selected as the site for one of Wingate's strongholds, from where the Chindits would wreak havoc on the Japanese within their area of operations. Calvert's troops won the engagement and received reinforcements and supplies by air to fortify the stronghold. Fire zones, barbed-wire belts, mines and bunkers with Vickers machine guns and 3in. mortars were constructed along with a light-plane airstrip for the evacuation of casualties. This stronghold became known as 'White City', because all material and

White City's light plane airstrip for the evacuation of the wounded. Later, a field to accommodate Dakota transports was built for larger deliveries and reinforcements. (IWM, SE 7937)

The crew of a 40mm Bofors anti-aircraft gun helps defend a jungle airstrip in Burma. (IWM, SE 928)

armaments had to be initially parachuted in and large numbers of parachutes clung to the jungle's trees. Since White City was located astride major Japanese road and rail communications, it became a magnet for Japanese attacks, which Calvert's troops repeatedly fought off. Over a week into the defence of White City, an airstrip was built to accommodate transport aircraft, which delivered six Bofors 40mm anti-aircraft artillery pieces, 2-pdr anti-tank guns and a battery of 25-pdr field artillery pieces. On 17 April, the Japanese made their last assault on White City, which was repelled. The use of aerial resupply would later become widespread among Fourteenth Army during its successful campaign in Burma.

Operation *Thursday*, the defence of White City, March–April 1944

On 16 March, the Chindits won a furious hand-to-hand combat engagement at Henu, north of the railhead at Mawlu. Henu was perfect for a Wingate 'stronghold' to block the Japanese road and railway supply of Northern Burma. It became known to Wingate's Air Commando pilots as White City since a large number of parachutes were festooning the jungle vegetation because all supply had to be initially air-dropped in. Over a week into the defence of White City, six Bofors 40mm anti-aircraft guns were air-transported in. The jungle vegetation with its clinging white parachutes was interspersed with cleared areas to house bunkers as well as sandbag and log-encased pits for the Bofors guns, which were vital to defend White City from ceaseless air attack. On an extremely heavy air raid on 7 April, as shown opposite, the Bofors gun crews claimed six certain and six probable Japanese medium bombers shot down. Jungle air supply and reinforcement had been perfected by Wingate's Chindits and its Air Commando under Wavell's tutelage.

Despite Churchill's enthusiasm for Wingate's operations and tactical approach, the cumulative failures in the Far East, especially in the Arakan, drove Churchill to look for ways of removing Wavell as C-in-C India. On 14 June 1943, Wavell was offered the Viceroyalty of India with Auchinleck once again taking over from him.

OPPOSING COMMANDERS

In February 1939, Wavell delivered the Lees Knowles Lectures at Cambridge entitled 'Generals and Generalship'. High-ranking members of the Wehrmacht held these speeches in high regard. Wilhelm Keitel, Hitler's Chief of the Oberkommando der Wehrmacht, wrote in the year the lectures were delivered: 'In the British Army today, there is only one good general [Wavell], but he is incomparably good. The others have no proper conception of the direction of mechanised war, but this officer, from 1928 onward, has studied the subject, and he may well prove the dominant personality in any war within the next five years.'

Wavell was to demonstrate his military personality to a vast assortment of opposing commanders on a wide array of fronts and theatres. These opponents were initially Italian but thereafter followed very able German officers, the most famous being Erwin Rommel. Also, during Wavell's Middle East Command, he fought political and religious leaders in Iraq and the Vichy French in Syria. Upon transfer to C-in-C India in June 1941, Wavell was soon to contest formidable opponents in the IJA with major setbacks throughout the short-lived ABDA campaign, principally for the British forces engaged in Malaya, Singapore, Burma and Hong Kong.

Generalfeldmarschall Erwin Rommel

Erwin Rommel was Wavell's principal opponent in the Western Desert. Rommel carried a copy of the German translation of Wavell's Lees Knowles Lectures and even annotated them. During the battles in Cyrenaica, the lectures were always on Rommel's person. Rommel's forte was mobile tactics, while his strategic sense could be erratic. Rommel's main attributes were his boundless energy, despite bouts of illness that were to plague him, and the power to sustain the initiative when other commanders would have sought disengagement. This tenacity of purpose, along with his innovative use of ad hoc formations, coupled with his ceaseless presence at the front to exhort his junior commanders and troops made him an extremely formidable opponent for Wavell.

Erwin Rommel was born on 15 November 1891 in Swabia, a region of southern Germany. Both his father and grandfather were teachers and there was no military tradition in the Rommel family. However, while very young, Rommel decided on a career in the army. On 19 July 1910, he entered the army as an officer-cadet in Infanterie-Regiment König Wilhelm I

(6. Württembergisches) Nr. 124. In the spring of 1911, he was sent to the War School at Danzig. Upon graduation in 1912, he became a *Leutnant*. In August 1914, when war erupted in Europe, Rommel commanded a horse-drawn artillery platoon. He was wounded several times while attacking a French position in late 1914. In this regard, his early officer years resembled Wavell's, who was also severely wounded in 1915 on the Western Front. He returned to his regiment after recuperating from his wounds in January 1915 only to be wounded again some months later.

After convalescence, Rommel was given command of a company in the elite Württembergisches Gebirgs-Bataillon in 1915 and stayed with this unit through to January 1918. His feats of military leadership and daring became legend while fighting the Italians in the Alps in October 1917 and he was promoted to *Hauptmann*, receiving the Pour le Merite decoration. As one of Germany's most decorated and astute young officers, Rommel was allowed to remain in the post-Versailles Treaty army, the Reichsheer. Promotion was painfully slow as in most post-war armies, and Rommel only achieved the rank of major in 1932. He commanded different battalions through 1935, when he became an instructor and course commandant at the Potsdam War School, reaching the rank of *Oberst* in August 1937. Like Wavell, Rommel was a writer penning his first book *Infantry in the Attack* in 1936. Adolf Hitler read the German bestseller and, after meeting Rommel, assigned him to command his security forces. In November 1938, Rommel assumed command of the War School at Wiener Neustadt near Vienna. However, he was summoned quickly to Berlin to take charge of Hitler's personal bodyguard as war clouds loomed during the summer of 1939. Hitler promoted the commander of his bodyguard to *Generalmajor*.

When war broke out, Rommel personally accompanied Hitler to Poland and saw Guderian's blitzkrieg tactics first-hand. Although an infantryman for his entire career, he realized the importance of armoured warfare. After the Polish campaign, Rommel asked Hitler for command of a Panzer division. To the amazement of his fellow officers, who knew that Rommel was a novice in armoured warfare, he was given the 7. Panzer-Division in February 1940, during the 'Phony War'. This was not an elite division, with over half of the tanks being the lighter models recently taken from the Czechs. Rommel trained this division incessantly and when the invasion of France and the Low Countries started on 10 May 1940, his division smashed through the Ardennes and across the Meuse River at Dinant. It then raced across France and Belgium so quickly that it received the soubriquet the 'Ghost Division'. On 21 May, Rommel faced Gort's only armoured counterattack at Arras and, with the help of anti-aircraft artillery, he was able to repel the British Matilda tanks as they closed to within 50 yards (45m) of his position. During this campaign, Rommel's division suffered 30 per cent casualties; however,

Generalfeldmarschall Erwin Rommel, Commander of the Deutches Afrika Korps (DAK) and later Panzerarmee Afrika. Rommel frustrated Wavell's early gains by retaking Cyrenaica and threatening Egypt. (IWM, GER 1281)

Generalmajor Kurt Student, commander of Fliegerkorps XI and founder of the German airborne forces. His plans and troops drove the British and Commonwealth troops from Crete, but at a heavy price in casualties. (IWM, HU 32007)

it captured almost 100,000 prisoners, including many of the British 51st Highland Division. On a more personal level, German Minister of Propaganda Joseph Goebbels ensured that Rommel received adulations in the German press and other media.

In February 1941, while on leave, he was again summoned by Hitler. On arrival, he was briefed on the Italian debacle in North Africa. To prevent the British evicting the Italians from North Africa, Hitler decided to send 5. leichte-Division and 15. Panzer-Division to Tripoli. Rommel would be the first commander of the newly formed Deutsches Afrika Korps, being promoted to *Generalleutnant* on 1 February 1941.

Generalmajor Kurt Student

Student was the founder of the German airborne force and was the major force behind the planning and implementation of Operation *Mercur*, the assault on Crete in May 1941. Student was a career soldier who had served as a *Leutnant* in a *Jäger* battalion before World War I. However, during World War I, he became an aviator flying first against the Russians and then over the Western Front. He was shot down in 1917 and severely wounded. Like Rommel, he saw his country's military arm severed almost completely by the Treaty of Versailles with German military aviation being completely banned. Flying commercial planes as a cover, Student was among a group of aviators who kept the air force spirit alive until Hitler and Göring violated the restrictions of the Treaty in 1933 and unveiled the Luftwaffe. Student was ambitious, extremely able and ruthless in pursuit of his goals. Again, like Rommel, he was an officer who led from the front and exhibited no fear for danger. Unsurprisingly, Student was able to easily convince Göring that airborne operations needed to be solely under the control of the Luftwaffe and Student was formally tasked with the creation of airborne formations on 4 June 1938.

Student assembled a variety of units and formed the 7. Flieger-Division in the face of antagonism and lack of cooperation from the regular army. However, Student was undaunted and proceeded to form a second *Fallschirmjäger* regiment in 1939. Well-honed and highly trained, Student's parachutists emerged as an elite fighting force and, once on the ground, would be able to fight like conventional infantry utilizing customary weaponry as well as small arms specific to their airborne mission.

Since the conquest of Poland was so quick, there was no opportunity for Student's paratroops to be deployed. However, they were employed in the invasions of Norway and Denmark, and during the invasion of France and the Low Countries, Student's parachutists took the Belgian fortress of Eben-Emael by a *coup de main*; as well as seizing bridges over the Albert Canal. In Holland, the paratroops were given the task of capturing a number of Dutch airfields intact. However, determined Dutch resistance foiled the paratroops' attempts to capture and maintain control over the airfields to facilitate later waves of planes and gliders bringing in reinforcements. Although the primary mission failed, the paratroops engaged a considerable numbers of Dutch soldiers.

In the invasion of Greece, the bridge across the Corinth Canal was a principal target for glider-borne paratroops, but an unforeseen event caused the bridge's span to blow and German casualties were high. However, the vertical envelopment of Crete was to be the pinnacle of Student's development of airborne operations. Owing to the extremely high casualty rate, it was also the final airborne mission authorized by Hitler.

Maresciallo Rodolfo Graziani, Commander-in-Chief Italian Forces in Libya

On 28 June 1940, Maresciallo Italo Balbo, the Libyan C-in-C, was shot down on his way back to North Africa from Rome. Balbo was replaced by Maresciallo Rodolfo Graziani. After having slaughtered Senussi Arabs in their rebellion in the early 1930s, he won the dubious nickname 'Butcher of the Fezzan' and in 1936, Graziani served as the Viceroy of Ethiopia; however, his level of brutality against the indigenous population was so severe that he was recalled and replaced by the Duke of Aosta in 1937. Graziani's enthusiasm for an invasion of Egypt during the summer of 1940 was not high. Fighting Arab insurgents with muzzle-loaders was relatively straightforward, but despite Graziani's vast superiority in numbers combating the British Western Desert Force, which was well equipped with modern weapons and armour, was a completely different level of conflict. Graziani's reluctance to invade Egypt was also based on sound logistical concerns. He told the Foreign Minister, Count Ciano, 'The water supply is entirely insufficient. We move towards a defeat, which in the desert, must inevitably develop into a total disaster'. This lack of leadership explains some of the absence of élan in the Italian Tenth Army's advance across the Egyptian frontier. Ultimately, Graziani was given an ultimatum by Mussolini, who threatened to replace him if he would not do as ordered.

During the initial advance, the constant pressure applied by the British led Graziani to disbelieve his own intelligence reports concerning British weakness in terms of numbers, which in part explains his slow pace and his decision to halt and order his men to fortify their positions, where Operation *Compass* would find them. Graziani wanted to build up sufficient fuel and ammunition dumps along his path of advance, but by the winter of 1940, Graziani had not advanced the Italian front line at all. He had merely built a series of little forts around Sidi Barrani and showed no desire to leave his redoubts.

The Duke of Aosta

Prince Amedeo, the Duke of Aosta, was a cousin of the King of Italy. He was chivalrous, cultured and a noted Anglophile for which reasons, among others, he was not well liked by Mussolini. The Duke of Aosta had been the

Governor-General of Italian East Africa and Viceroy of Ethiopia since 1937. He was chosen to replace Graziani in Italian East Africa when the latter's practices were deemed barbaric and harmful to relations with the native inhabitants. However, Mussolini also regarded him as lacking in ruthlessness and commanding military ability. He surrendered with remnants of his army on 17 May 1941, in part to prevent a massacre of the wounded, and died in captivity in Kenya in 1942.

Amin el-Huseini, the Grand Mufti of Jerusalem

El-Huseini the Grand Mufti of Jerusalem, provided the major support for the Iraqi Prime Minister Rashid Ali el-Gailani after he was successful in his *coup d'état*. The Grand Mufti had previously escaped to Baghdad in 1939 after Wavell had successfully suppressed the Arab Rebellion in Palestine. A bitter Anglophobe and anti-Zionist, the Grand Mufti received the support of Hitler and the German military machine. Despite his defeat in Iraq at the hands of Wavell's expedition to relieve the besieged RAF bases, el-Huseini was taken under the protection of the Nazis and fomented Muslim hatred in the Balkans against the enemies of the Third Reich.

Imperial Japanese Army generals

Lieutenant General Renya Mutaguchi commanded the formidable Fifteenth Army. He is described as a 'heavy-bodied, bullet-headed officer with hard eyes and thick lips who fiercely overrode the intractable problem of supply and whose wrath was so feared by his staff that they did not press their doubts'.

In Burma, Mutaguchi operated from his HQ in Maymyo in the very buildings where Stilwell had met Alexander, Wavell and Wingate at the start of the retreat in 1942. Mutaguchi had under his command the 18th Division led by General Shinichi Tanaka, which faced General Joseph Stilwell in the north; the 56th Division facing Chiang Kai-Shek's Yoke Force in the east; and the 33rd Division facing the British on the Chindwin River. Tanaka was also among the conquerors of Singapore, Malaya, and Burma. The British senior commanders in Delhi may have been derisive and willing to ignore any important outcome of Wingate's first Chindit expedition in March 1943 (Operation *Longcloth*), but Mutaguchi later conceded that it had changed his entire strategic thinking. Wingate had shown that it was possible for units to attack across the main north–south grain of the rivers and mountains of Burma. This information, along with intelligence of the British build-up at Imphal, convinced Mutaguchi that he must attack Imphal and Kohima to pre-empt another British offensive from being launched from India in 1944. Mutaguchi was certain where he had to concentrate his attack and that was India, so he ordered Lieutenant-General Kotuku Sato to launch his 31st Division against the British garrison at Kohima. On 11 April 1944, Mutaguchi was relieved of the responsibility of looking after northern Burma and was given the single task of the Imphal/Kohima offensive. Imperial General Japanese Headquarters established the 33rd Army under Lieutenant-General

Masaki Honda. He took over 18th Division, 56th Division, the 24th Independent Mixed Brigade and the 53rd Division now arriving in Burma.

Mutaguchi planned a three-division attack into India, Operation *U-Go*: the 33rd Division under General Yanagida to advance towards Imphal from the south against 17th Indian Division, which had fought in the retreat from Burma but was now substantially retrained and re-equipped; 15th Division under General Yamauchi, together with units of the Indian National Army recruited from Indian prisoners of war, to attack Imphal in two prongs from the east; and, most significantly; 31st Division under General Sato, which was to advance to Dimapur, the huge supply base, 11 miles long and 1 mile wide (17 by 2km), which provided for the whole of Slim's Fourteenth Army. Mutaguchi intended that as soon as Kohima and Dimapur were captured, his victorious forces, accompanied by the Indian National Army and its leader, Subhas Chandra Bose, would advance into Bengal, where the subjugated Indian populace would mount an insurrection against British rule and support his triumphant March on Delhi.

If this campaign of March–June 1944 had succeeded, British and American forces operating in Burma would have had all contact with the west severed. Faulty logistic and supply arrangements, coupled with the selfless bravery of Indian and British troops thwarted his *U-Go* plan. Mutaguchi had started his offensive with only one month's rations and supplies in anticipation of capturing the stores at Dimapur, and a lack of supplies caused the downfall of the plan.

Mountbatten, as Supreme Commander SEAC, had made the decision to transfer 30 supply aircraft from the 'Hump' operation to airlift 5th Indian Division back from the Arakan to bolster the defences of Kohima and Dimapur and enable Slim's victory. There is little doubt that the airlift of 5th Indian Division played a vital role in the survival of Kohima and Dimapur, thereby depriving Mutaguchi of his prizes. Mutaguchi had sacked his three divisional generals in the course of Operation *U-Go*. Once it failed, he was next to go and on 30 August 1944 he was transferred to the General Staff in Tokyo.

INSIDE THE MIND

Archibald Wavell blended military leadership with scholarship and his campaigns possessed the twin personality traits of cunning and deception, coupled with a leaning towards the unorthodox. As a biographer of Allenby and a historian chronicling his campaigns in Palestine during World War I, it is clear that it was Wavell's staff service under his desert mentor that inculcated Allenby's approach to warfare into his own mind.

Wavell nurtured a generation of junior officers and made certain that as his acolytes rose through the ranks, they would be supported in their cultivation of new methods of warfare. He also set up a suitable command structure

Wavell at a conference in New Delhi, 1943. Among those also present are General 'Hap' Arnold, Lieutenant-General Joseph Stilwell and General Sir John Dill. (United States Army Military Heritage Institute)

to implement these techniques. The names of Wingate, O'Connor, Clarke, Bagnold, Dorman-Smith and Simonds, along with their military innovations, are for ever associated with Wavell's tutelage. Assessing the methods and effectiveness of these officers provides a unique glimpse into the inner mechanics of Wavell's mind. From a different perspective, which officer within the inner circle of either Rommel or Montgomery acquired the necessary support and then the limelight to exhibit their military talent?

Despite Wavell's personal attributes and devotion to military duty, he stands behind such figures as Rommel or Montgomery as a 'consummate professional soldier'. Although harsh, Wavell's own words echo this critical comparison: 'The main ethical objection to war for intelligent people is that it is so deplorably dull and usually so inefficiently run.... War is a wasteful, boring, muddled affair; and people of fine intelligence either resign themselves to it or fret badly, especially if they are near the heart of things and can see matters which ought to be done, or done better, and cannot contrive to get them set right.' Wavell was no dilettante, but he lacked the single-minded purpose that drove contemporaries such as Rommel or Montgomery.

One aspect of Wavell's character that stands out in sharp contrast to many other successful commanders was his humility. The origin of this trait seems to date back to his preparatory school days. Wavell's biographer Connell noted that 'he was a little suspicious of his intellectual capacity, and to a remarkable degree he kept his own counsel. He maintained this reserve all his life, and combined it with a permanent habit of self-depreciation.' Perhaps, this helps to explain some of his reticence in debate and tacit posture when confronted by Churchill in person or by cable.

One of the major problems Wavell faced was Churchill's underestimation of his capabilities, which was exacerbated by the Prime Minister's constant interference with his command. The relationship between Churchill and Wavell was very difficult, primarily because of their different temperaments. Wavell's silences led the Prime Minister to conclude that there was little to him. However, both were historians and gifted writers. Twice, Churchill would remove Wavell and then twice re-employ him, the second time as Viceroy of India, with a peerage.

In May 1940, Churchill directed the CIGS to redeploy eight regular battalions from the Middle East to assist with Britain's home defences. With war threatening in the Middle East, Wavell opposed the redeployment and was supported in this action by the CIGS. While Churchill dropped the matter, he never forgot Wavell's opposition and this clouded their relationship from the start. In July 1940, the Prime Minister increasingly meddled with Wavell's Middle East theatre. Because Wavell kept his own counsel, not even the Prime Minister was initially taken into his confidence during the planning stages of Operation *Compass*. Churchill was clear that Wavell was to waste no chance to cross swords with the Italians after their declaration of war in June 1940, in order to impress Britain's combativeness upon the neutral powers.

In August 1940, during consultations with Churchill and the Defence Committee in London, the extreme differences in personality between the two helped foster a direct conflict. As Connell again noted, 'At this supreme moment in his personal drama Churchill met, in Wavell, a man of the highest moral and intellectual stature, with a great military reputation, holding a post whose responsibilities and challenges were similar though no greater than his own, who for reasons which neither of them fully comprehended was incapable of playing the part in that drama that

Churchill with members of the Middle East War Council in Cairo in August 1942. Wavell is standing in the back row, third from right. Auchinleck, standing next to Wavell, was shortly to be relieved as C-in-C, Middle East Command. (IWM, E 15218)

Wavell, as Viceroy of India, presenting Victoria Crosses to two of his Indian Army soldiers. (IWM, MWY 49)

Churchill wished him to play.' Wavell's strengths were in his written skills, thus his sombre side did not project him well as a confident commander to the ever-glib Churchill. At the August 1940 consultation Wavell's 'almost pathologic taciturnity' irritated Churchill deeply, since the Prime Minister believed this characteristic demonstrated a passivity that would be exhibited on the battlefield. Dill, the CIGS, begged Wavell, 'Talk to him, Archie'; however, during these conferences, Wavell went deeper into his shell. As Churchill learned, a quiet demeanour hid a bold, decisive, offensive-minded commander as Wavell was to prove with Operation *Compass*. Unfortunately, Wavell left London with the clear feeling that he did not enjoy Churchill's full confidence, even though Churchill was willing to provide scarce resources to Wavell at a period when Britain still faced the possible threat of German invasion.

Throughout the war, Churchill continually failed to appreciate the administrative difficulties of modern desert warfare and of the significant manpower requirements for internal security in the Middle East. During the remainder of Wavell's tenure of command, Churchill was to question him on the employment of the 350,000 men in the Middle East theatre continually. This problem, coupled with Wavell's later mistakes in conducting the campaign, was to lead to his eventual dismissal.

WHEN WAR IS DONE

Viceroy of India

In January 1943 Wavell was promoted to field marshal. Later that year, he was created Viscount Wavell of Cyrenaica and Winchester. Wavell also served as the 23rd Viceroy and Governor-General of India from 1 October 1943 until 21 February 1947. He believed that he should have been appointed the first Allied Supreme Commander for the South-East Asia theatre; however, after the ill-fated Arakan campaign of 1942–43, which Wavell believed was not supported properly from London, Mountbatten was appointed the Allied Supreme Commander for the theatre.

Eden's private secretary, Oliver Stanley, described Wavell as a 'funny choice' for Viceroy and the entire appointment process appeared to be designed by Churchill to keep Wavell out of the public limelight in Britain. Others claimed more cynically that Wavell received the position either by chance or default. In any event at a dinner with the Prime Minister on 14 June 1943, Churchill informed him that he was to be the next Viceroy and that 'you will have to become a civilian, and put off your uniform'.

Wavell had no prior experience that made him any more qualified than previous British diplomats in dealing with increasingly fervent Indian Nationalists. In addition, Wavell and Churchill held differing views on India's quest for independence. During his previous service in India, Wavell had been an active participant in Indian politics at the local level. In contrast to Churchill, he harboured more liberal leanings towards the nationalists and favoured early planning for independence. However, Churchill was not seriously interested in such nationalist talk and disagreed with Wavell's effusive praise

Wavell, as Viceroy of India, presents an award to a member of the Royal Norfolk Regiment, 2nd Indian Division.
(IWM, SE 2862)

of Allenby's liberalism as High Commissioner in Egypt from 1919 to 1922, emphasized in the publication of the life of his mentor published in London in the autumn of 1943. There was concern that Wavell's biography of Allenby might provoke anger in the Conservative Party in Britain, to which Wavell noted in his journal, 'I don't think I mind if it does, I am not very much in sympathy with the right-wing Conservative'. Wavell made a curious entry in a formal note dated 20 August 1943, several weeks after having been notified of his forthcoming appointment as Viceroy of India: 'I have been turning over in my mind how I should approach this question of finding a solution of the Indian problem if I discarded all normal methods and trusted entirely to my own common sense (such as it is) and my previous experience and training. As a result I have evolved the following scenario, on which I invite your opinion. It will certainly appear to you as fantastical, impossible or inadvisable. I have always been in military matters an upholder of unorthodox methods when orthodox methods have failed, as I think they have in India.' As Lewin notes, here was Wavell 'reviving that spirit of calculated originality which characterized his early ideas about *Compass* and, indeed, flickered to life intermittently during his reign as Commander-in-Chief, India'.

Akin to his planning for Operation *Compass*, Wavell wanted to invite a select group of India's leaders, including Gandhi, Nehru and Jinnah, to a conference in Delhi 'under conditions of extreme secrecy'. Again, his thoughts for propelling India to self-governance were firmly embedded within an intellectual plan rather than an expedient, political one. Wavell's desire was to guarantee for His Majesty's Government that India would be granted independence as soon as possible after the war was won. Churchill, the quintessential Victorian and defender of the Empire, rejected Wavell's approach outright.

Although he performed well as Viceroy during the Bengal famine of 1943, and was initially popular with both Indian politicians and India's emerging generation of business leaders, his effectiveness was hampered by the internecine conflict between the various Indian political factions. After the end of the war, Wavell found himself at odds with Attlee's Labour Party as well. Wavell appeared to ally himself, intellectually at least, with the Muslim League while Attlee's government was mainly interested in working with Nehru's Congress Party. Wavell did attempt to bring both major factions together in a united coalition at the Simla Conference of July 1945, but, once again, the recurrent theme of lack of support from London hampered his attempts to allow the British to exit the Raj and let the Indians govern themselves.

Eventually, Prime Minister Clement Attlee replaced Wavell with only one month's notice rather than the usual six-month interval. Ironically, it was Mountbatten who was appointed as Viceroy in 1947, just as he had received the title of Supreme Allied Commander South-East Asia Command that Wavell had truly desired. Mountbatten later championed many of Wavell's ideas and schedules for British withdrawal and Indian partition along religious lines.

Wavell returned to England in 1947 and was named the High Steward of Colchester and created Earl Wavell, receiving the title of Viscount Keren of Eritrea and Winchester. From March 1946, Wavell had also served as colonel of the Black Watch. In the spring of 1950 he came down with jaundice, and was critically ill in hospital for three weeks before passing away on 24 May 1950.

A LIFE IN WORDS

'Fate did not spare the great Lord Wavell time to write his memoirs', Bernard Fergusson, a member of the Black Watch and a Chindit column leader, wrote in *Wavell: Portrait of a Soldier* in 1961. 'It is fully in character that while the reminiscences of other higher commanders have been pouring from the presses his own voice should still be silent; during all the ill luck that befell him, and after, he never spoke in his own defence.' Since Wavell's death in May 1950 dozens of books have praised him, though Winston Churchill's six-volume *The Second World War*, which appeared in 1950, offers a mixed opinion. After the Prime Minister had summoned Wavell to London for 'severe' discussions in early August 1940, Churchill wrote,